CliffsNotes™

Things Fall Apart

By John Chua and Suzanne Pavlos, M.Ed., C.S.W.

IN THIS BOOK

- Learn about the Life and Background of the Author

- Preview an Introduction to the Novel

- Explore themes, character development, and recurring images in the Critical Commentaries

- Examine in-depth Character Analyses

- Acquire an understanding of the novel with Critical Essays

- Reinforce what you learn with CliffsNotes Review

- Find additional information to further your study in CliffsNotes Resource Center and online at www.cliffsnotes.com

WILEY

Wiley Publishing, Inc.

About the Author

John Chua has written for a wide variety of media, including television. He has written three Cliffs-Notes and holds a BA from Knox College and an MBA from the University of Illinois. Suzanne Pavlos taught high school English and reading. She is currently a freelance writer and editor and working as a psychotherapist.

Publisher's Acknowledgments

Editorial

Project Editor: Linda Brandon

Acquisitions Editor: Greg Tubach

Copy Editor: Mary Fales

Glossary Editors: The editors and staff at Webster's New World™ Dictionaries

Editorial Administrator: Michelle Hacker

Editorial Assistant: Jennifer Young

Composition

Indexer: York Production Services, Inc.

Proofreader: York Production Services, Inc.

Wiley Indianapolis Composition Services

CliffsNotes™ *Things Fall Apart*
Published by:
Wiley Publishing, Inc.
111 River Street
Hoboken, NJ 07030
www.wiley.com

Table of Contents

How to Use This Book

This CliffsNotes study guide on Achebe's *Things Fall Apart* supplements the original literary work, giving you background information about the author, an introduction to the work, a graphical character map, critical commentaries, expanded glossaries, and a comprehensive index, all for you to use as an educational tool that will allow you to better understand *Things Fall Apart*. This study guide was written with the assumption that you have read *Things Fall Apart*. Reading a literary work doesn't mean that you immediately grasp the major themes and devices used by the author; this study guide will help supplement your reading to be sure you get all you can from Achebe's *Things Fall Apart*. CliffsNotes Review tests your comprehension of the original text and reinforces learning with questions and answers, practice projects, and more. For further information on Chinua Achebe and *Things Fall Apart*, check out the CliffsNotes Resource Center.

CliffsNotes provides the following icons to highlight essential elements of particular interest:

Reveals the underlying themes in the work.

Helps you to more easily relate to or discover the depth of a character.

Uncovers such elements as setting, atmosphere, mystery, passion, violence, irony, symbolism, tragedy, foreshadowing, and satire.

Enables you to appreciate the nuances of words and phrases.

Don't Miss Our Web Site

Discover classic literature as well as modern-day treasures by visiting the CliffsNotes Web site at www.cliffsnotes.com. You can obtain a quick download of a CliffsNotes title, purchase a title in print form, browse our catalog, or view online samples.

You'll also find interactive tools that are fun and informative, links to interesting Web sites, tips, articles, and additional helpful resources not only for literature but for test prep, finance, careers, computers, and the Internet, too. See you at www.cliffsnotes.com!

LIFE AND BACKGROUND OF THE AUTHOR

The following abbreviated biography of Chinua Achebe is provided so that you might become more familiar with his life and the historical times that possibly influenced his writing. Read this Life and Background of the Author section and recall it when reading Achebe's *Things Fall Apart*, thinking of any thematic relationship between Achebe's work and his life.

Personal Background

Chinua Achebe (pronounced *Chee*-noo-ah Ah-*chay*-bay) is considered by many critics and teachers to be the most influential African writer of his generation. His writings, including the novel *Things Fall Apart*, have introduced readers throughout the world to creative uses of language and form, as well as to factual inside accounts of modern African life and history. Not only through his literary contributions but also through his championing of bold objectives for Nigeria and Africa, Achebe has helped reshape the perception of African history, culture, and place in world affairs.

The first novel of Achebe's, *Things Fall Apart*, is recognized as a literary classic and is taught and read everywhere in the English-speaking world. The novel has been translated into at least forty-five languages and has sold several million copies. A year after publication, the book won the Margaret Wong Memorial Prize, a major literary award.

Achebe was born in the Igbo (formerly spelled *Ibo*) town of Ogidi in eastern Nigeria on November 16, 1930, the fifth child of Isaiah Okafor Achebe and Janet Iloegbunam Achebe. His father was an instructor in Christian catechism for the Church Missionary Society. Nigeria was a British colony during Achebe's early years, and educated English-speaking families like the Achebes occupied a privileged position in the Nigerian power structure. His parents even named him Albert, after Prince Albert, the husband of Queen Victoria of Great Britain. (Achebe himself chose his Igbo name when he was in college.)

Education

Achebe attended the Church Missionary Society's school where the primary language of instruction for the first two years was Igbo. At about eight, he began learning English. His relatively late introduction to English allowed Achebe to develop a sense of cultural pride and an appreciation of his native tongue—values that may not have been cultivated had he been raised and taught exclusively in English. Achebe's home fostered his understanding of both cultures: He read books in English in his father's library, and he spent hours listening to his mother and sister tell traditional Igbo stories.

At fourteen, Achebe was selected to attend the Government College in Umuahia, the equivalent of a university preparatory school and considered the best in West Africa. Achebe excelled at his studies, and after graduating at eighteen, he was accepted to study medicine at the new University College at Ibadan, a member college of London University at the time. The demand for educated Nigerians in the government was heightened because Nigeria was preparing for self-rule and independence. Only with a college degree was a Nigerian likely to enter the higher ranks of the civil service.

The growing nationalism in Nigeria was not lost on Achebe. At the university, he dropped his English name "Albert" in favor of the Igbo name "Chinua," short for Chinualumogo. Just as Igbo names in *Things Fall Apart* have literal meanings, Chinualumogo is translated as "My spirit come fight for me."

At University College, Achebe switched his studies to liberal arts, including history, religion, and English. His first published stories appeared in the student publication the *University Herald*. These stories have been reprinted in the collection *Girls at War and Other Stories*, which was published in 1972. Of his student writings, only a few are significantly relative to his more mature works; short stories such as "Marriage is a Private Affair" and "Dead Man's Path" explore the conflicts that arise when Western culture meets African society.

Career Highlights

After graduating with a Bachelor of Arts degree in 1953, Achebe joined the Nigerian Broadcasting Corporation as a producer of radio talks. In 1956, he went to London to attend the British Broadcasting Corporation (BBC) Staff School. While in London, he submitted the manuscript for *Things Fall Apart* to a publisher, with the encouragement and support of one of his BBC instructors, a writer and literary critic. The novel was published in 1958 by Heinemann, a publishing firm that began a long relationship with Achebe and his work. Fame came almost instantly. Achebe has said that he never experienced the life of a struggling writer.

Upon returning to Nigeria, Achebe rose rapidly within the Nigerian Broadcasting Corporation. As founder and director of the Voice of Nigeria in 1961, Achebe and his colleagues aimed at developing more national identity and unity through radio programs that highlighted Nigerian affairs and culture.

Political Problems

Turmoil in Nigeria from 1966 to 1972 was matched by turmoil for Achebe. In 1966, young Igbo officers in the Nigerian army staged a coup d'ètat. Six months later, another coup by non-Igbo officers overthrew the Igbo-led government. The new government targeted Achebe for persecution, knowing that his views were unsympathetic to the new regime. Achebe fled to Nsukka in eastern Nigeria, which is predominantly Igbo-speaking, and he became a senior research fellow at the University of Nigeria, Nsukka. In 1967, the eastern part of Nigeria declared independence as the nation of Biafra. This incident triggered thirty months of civil war that ended only when Biafra was defeated. Achebe then fled to Europe and America, where he wrote and talked about Biafran affairs.

Later Writing

Like many other African writers, Achebe believes that artistic and literary works must deal primarily with the problems of society. He has said that "art is, and always was, at the service of man" rather than an end in itself, accountable to no one. He believes that "any good story, any good novel, should have a message, should have a purpose."

Continuing his relationship with Heinemann, Achebe published four other novels: *No Longer at Ease* (the 1960 sequel to *Things Fall Apart*), *Arrow of God* (1964), *A Man of the People* (1966), and *Anthills of the Savannah* (1987). He also wrote and published several children's books that express his basic views in forms and language understandable to young readers.

In his later books, Achebe confronts the problems faced by Nigeria and other newly independent African nations. He blames the nation's problems on the lack of leadership in Nigeria since its independence. In 1983, he published *The Trouble with Nigeria*, a critique of corrupt politicians in his country. Achebe has also published two collections of short stories and three collections of essays. He is the founding editor of Heinemann's African Writers series; the founder and publisher of *Uwa Ndi Igbo: A Bilingual Journal of Igbo Life and Arts*; and the editor of the magazine *Okike*, Nigeria's leading journal of new writing.

Teaching

In addition to his writing career, Achebe has maintained an active teaching career. In 1972, he was appointed to a three-year visiting professorship at the University of Massachusetts at Amherst and, in 1975, to a one-year visiting professorship at the University of Connecticut. In 1976, with matters sufficiently calm in Nigeria, he returned as professor of English at the University of Nigeria, Nsukka, with which he had been affiliated since 1966. In 1990, he became the Charles P. Stevenson, Jr., professor of literature at Bard College, Annandale, New York.

Literary Awards

Achebe has received many awards from academic and cultural institutions around the world. In 1959, he won the Margaret Wong Memorial Prize for *Things Fall Apart*. The following year, after the publication of its sequel, *No Longer At Ease*, he was awarded the Nigerian National Trophy for Literature. His book of poetry, *Christmas in Biafra*, written during the Nigerian civil war, won the first Commonwealth Poetry Prize in 1972. More than twenty universities in Great Britain, Canada, Nigeria, and the United States have awarded Achebe honorary degrees.

INTRODUCTION TO THE NOVEL

The following Introduction section is provided solely as an educational tool and is not meant to replace the experience of your reading the work. Read the Introduction and A Brief Synopsis to enhance your understanding of the work and to prepare yourself for the critical thinking that should take place whenever you read any work of fiction or nonfiction. Keep the List of Characters and Character Map at hand so that as you read the original literary work, if you encounter a character about whom you're uncertain, you can refer to the List of Characters and Character Map to refresh your memory.

Introduction

Chinua Achebe's *Things Fall Apart* is probably the most authentic narrative ever written about life in Nigeria at the turn of the twentieth century. Although the novel was first published in 1958—two years before Nigeria achieved its independence—thousands of copies are still sold every year in the United States alone. Millions of copies have been sold around the world in its many translations. The novel has been adapted for productions on the stage, on the radio, and on television. Teachers in high schools, colleges, and graduate schools use the novel as a textbook in many types of classes—from history and social studies to comparative literature and anthropology.

The novel takes its title from a verse in the poem "The Second Coming" by W. B. Yeats, an Irish poet, essayist, and dramatist:

Turning and turning in the widening gyre

The falcon cannot hear the falconer;

Things fall apart; the center cannot hold;

Mere anarchy is loosed upon the world.

In this poem—ironically, a product of European thought—Yeats describes an apocalyptic vision in which the world collapses into anarchy because of an internal flaw in humanity. In *Things Fall Apart*, Achebe illustrates this vision by showing us what happened in the Igbo society of Nigeria at the time of its colonization by the British. Because of internal weaknesses within the native structure and the divided nature of Igbo society, the community of Umuofia in this novel is unable to withstand the tidal wave of foreign religion, commerce, technology, and government. In "The Second Coming," Yeats evokes the anti-Christ leading an anarchic world to destruction. This ominous tone gradually emerges in *Things Fall Apart* as an intrusive religious presence and an insensitive government together cause the traditional Umuofian world to fall apart.

Literary Purpose

When *Things Fall Apart* was first published, Achebe announced that one of his purposes was to present a complex, dynamic society to a Western audience who perceived African society as primitive, simple, and backward. Unless Africans could tell their side of their story, Achebe believed that the African experience would forever be "mistold," even by such well-meaning authors as Joyce Cary in *Mister Johnson*. Cary worked in Nigeria as a colonial administrator and was sympathetic to the Nigerian people. Yet Achebe feels that Cary, along with other Western writers such as Joseph Conrad, misunderstood Africa. Many European writers have presented the continent as a dark place inhabited by people with impenetrable, primitive minds; Achebe considers this reductionist portrayal of Africa racist. He points to Conrad, who wrote against imperialism but reduced Africans to mysterious, animalistic, and exotic "others." In an interview published in 1994, Achebe explains that his anger about the inaccurate portrayal of African culture by white colonial writers does not imply that students should not read works by Conrad or Cary. On the contrary, Achebe urges students to read such works in order to better understand the racism of the colonial era.

Achebe also kept in mind his own Nigerian people as an audience. In 1964, he stated his goal: "To help my society regain belief in itself and put away the complexes of the years of denigration and self-abasement. . . . I would be quite satisfied if my novels . . . did no more than teach my [African] readers that their past—with all its imperfections—was not one long night of savagery from which the first Europeans acting on God's behalf delivered them."

In *Things Fall Apart*, the Europeans' understanding of Africa is particularly exemplified in two characters: the Reverend James Smith and the unnamed District Commissioner. Mr. Smith sees no need to compromise on unquestionable religious doctrine or practices, even during their introduction to a society very different from his own. He simply does not recognize any benefit for allowing the Nigerians to retain elements of their heritage. The District Commissioner, on the other hand, prides himself on being a student of primitive customs and sees himself as a benevolent leader who has only the best intentions for pacifying the primitive tribes and bringing them into the modern era. Both men would express surprise if anyone suggested to them that their European values may not be entirely appropriate for these societies. The Commissioner's plan for briefly treating the story of Okonkwo illustrates the inclination toward Western simplification and essentialization of African culture.

To counter this inclination, Achebe brings to life an African culture with a religion, a government, a system of money, and an artistic tradition, as well as a judicial system. While technologically unsophisticated, the Igbo culture is revealed to the reader as remarkably complex. Furthermore, *Things Fall Apart* ironically reverses the style of novels by such writers as Conrad and Cary, who created flat and stereotypical African characters. Instead, Achebe stereotypes the white colonialists as rigid, most with imperialistic intentions, whereas the Igbos are highly individual, many of them open to new ideas.

But readers should note that Achebe is not presenting Igbo culture as faultless and idyllic. Indeed, Achebe would contest such a romantic portrayal of his native people. In fact, many Western writers who wrote about colonialism (including Joseph Conrad, George Orwell, Herman Melville, and Graham Greene) were opposed to imperialism but were romantic in their portrayal of noble savages—primitive and animalistic, yet uncorrupted and innocent. The opposition to imperialism that such authors voiced often rested on the notion that an advanced Western society corrupts and destroys the non-Western world. Achebe regards this notion as an unacceptable argument as well as a myth. The Igbos were not noble savages, and although the Igbo world was eventually destroyed, the indigenous culture was never an idyllic haven, even before the arrival of the white colonialists. In *Things Fall Apart*, Achebe depicts negative as well as positive elements of Igbo culture, and he is sometimes as critical of his own people as he is of the colonizers.

Achebe has been a major force in the worldwide literary movement to define and describe this African experience. Other postcolonial writers in this movement include Leopold Senghor, Wole Soyinka, Aime Cesaire, Derek Walcott, Ngugi wa Thiong'o, and Birago Diop. These writers not only confront a multiethnic perspective of history and truth, but they also challenge readers to reexamine themselves in this complex and evolving world.

As an African novel written in English and departing significantly from more familiar colonial writing, *Things Fall Apart* was a ground breaking work. Achebe's role in making modern African literature a part of world literature cannot be understated.

Note: Throughout this novel, Achebe uses the spelling *Ibo*, the old spelling of the Umuofian community. Throughout the CliffsNotes, the contemporary spelling *Igbo* is used.

A Brief History of Nigeria

The history of Nigeria is bound up with its geography. About one-third larger than the state of Texas, Nigeria is located above the inner curve of the elbow on the west coast of Africa, just north of the equator and south of the Sahara Desert. More than two hundred ethnic groups—each with its own language, beliefs, and culture—live in present-day Nigeria. The largest ethnic groups are the mostly Protestant Yoruba in the west, the Catholic Igbo in the east, and the predominantly Muslim Hausa-Fulani in the north. This diversity of peoples is the result of thousands of years of history; as traders, nomads, and refugees from invaders and climatic changes came to settle with the indigenous population, and as foreign nations became aware of the area's resources.

The events in *Things Fall Apart* take place at the end of the nineteenth century and in the early part of the twentieth century. Although the British did not occupy most of Nigeria until 1904, they had a strong presence in West Africa since the early nineteenth century. The British were a major buyer of African slaves in the seventeenth and eighteenth centuries.

In 1807, however, the British outlawed slave trade within their empire. At the time, they did not yet control Nigeria, and internal wars continually increased the available supply of captured slaves. In 1861, frustrated with the expanding slave trade, the British decided to occupy Lagos, a major slave-trading post and the capital of present-day Nigeria. Slowly and hesitantly, the British occupied the rest of Nigeria.

Ultimately, the British were prompted to occupy Nigeria for more than the slave trade. The British were in competition with other Europeans for control of the natural wealth of West Africa. At the Berlin Conference of 1884-85—a meeting arranged to settle rivalries among European powers—the British proclaimed Nigeria to be their territory. They bought palm oil, peanuts, rubber, cotton, and other agricultural products from the Nigerians. Indeed, trade in these products made some Nigerian traders very wealthy. In the early twentieth century, the British defined the collection of diverse ethnic groups as one country, Nigeria, and declared it a colony of the British Empire.

The British moved into Nigeria with a combination of government control, religious mission, and economic incentive. In the north, the British ruled indirectly, with the support of the local Muslim leaders, who collected taxes and administered a government on behalf of the British. In the south, however, where communities (such as Umuofia in *Things Fall Apart*) were often not under one central authority, the British had to intervene directly and forcefully to control the local population.

For example, a real-life tragedy at the community of Ahiara serves as the historical model for the massacre of the village of Abame in Chapter 15 of *Things Fall Apart*. On November 16, 1905, a white man rode his bicycle into Ahiara and was killed by the natives. A month later, an expedition of British forces searched the villages in the area and killed many natives in reprisal.

The Ahiara incident led to the Bende-Onitsha Hinterland Expedition, a force created to eliminate Igbo opposition. The British destroyed the powerful Awka Oracle and killed all opposing Igbo groups. In 1912, the British instituted the Collective Punishment Ordinance, which stipulated punishment against an entire village or community for crimes committed by one or more persons against the white colonialists.

The British operated an efficient administrative system and introduced a form of British culture to Nigeria. They also sent many capable young Nigerians to England for education. The experience of Nigerians who lived overseas in the years preceding, during, and after World War II gave rise to a class of young, educated nationalists who agitated for independence from Great Britain. The British agreed to the Nigerians' demands and, in 1947, instituted a ten-year economic plan toward independence. Nigeria became an independent country on October 1, 1960, and became a republic in 1963.

With the British long gone from Nigeria, corruption and a lack of leadership continued to hamper Nigeria's quest for true democracy. A series of military coups and dictatorships in the 1970s, 1980s, and early 1990s replaced the fragile democracy that Nigeria enjoyed in the early 1960s. In 1993, Nigeria held a democratic presidential election, which was followed by yet another bloodless coup. And so continues the political pattern for the troubled, violent, most populous country in Africa.

A Brief Synopsis

Things Fall Apart is about the tragic fall of the protagonist, Okonkwo, and the Igbo culture. Okonkwo is a respected and influential leader within the Igbo community of Umuofia in eastern Nigeria.

He first earns personal fame and distinction, and brings honor to his village, when he defeats Amalinze the Cat in a wrestling contest. Okonkwo determines to gain titles for himself and become a powerful and wealthy man in spite of his father's weaknesses.

Okonkwo's father, Unoka, was a lazy and wasteful man. He often borrowed money and then squandered it on palm-wine and merry-making with friends. Consequently, his wife and children often went hungry. Within the community, Unoka was considered a failure and a laughingstock. He was referred to as *agbala*, one who resembles the weakness of a woman and has no property. Unoka died a shameful death and left numerous debts.

Okonkwo despises and resents his father's gentle and idle ways. He resolves to overcome the shame that he feels as a result of his father's weaknesses by being what he considers to be "manly"; therefore, he dominates his wives and children by being insensitive and controlling.

Because Okonkwo is a leader of his community, he is asked to care for a young boy named Ikemefuna, who is given to the village as a peace offering by neighboring Mbaino to avoid war with Umuofia. Ikemefuna befriends Okonkwo's son, Nwoye, and Okonkwo becomes inwardly fond of the boy.

Over the years, Okonkwo becomes an extremely volatile man; he is apt to explode at the slightest provocation. He violates the Week of Peace when he beats his youngest wife, Ojiugo, because she went to braid her hair at a friend's house and forgot to prepare the afternoon meal and feed her children. Later, he severely beats and shoots a gun at his second wife, Ekwefi, because she took leaves from his banana plant to wrap food for the Feast of the New Yam.

After the coming of the locusts, Ogbuefi Ezeuder, the oldest man in the village, relays to Okonkwo a message from the Oracle. The Oracle says that Ikemefuna must be killed as part of the retribution for the Umuofian woman killed three years earlier in Mbaino. He tells Okonkwo not to partake in the murder, but Okonkwo doesn't listen. He feels that not participating would be a sign of weakness. Consequently, Okonkwo kills Ikemefuna with his machete. Nwoye realizes that his father has murdered Ikemefuna and begins to distance himself from his father and the clansmen.

Okonkwo becomes depressed after killing Ikemefuna, so he visits his best friend, Obierika, who disapproves of his role in Ikemefuna's killing. Obierika says that Okonkwo's act will upset the Earth and the earth goddess will seek revenge. After discussing Ikemefuna's death with Obierika, Okonkwo is finally able to sleep restfully, but he is awakened by his wife Ekwefi. Their daughter Ezinma, whom Okonkwo is fond of, is dying. Okonkwo gathers grasses, barks, and leaves to prepare medicine for Ezinma.

A public trial is held on the village commons. Nine clan leaders, including Okonkwo, represent the spirits of their ancestors. The nine clan leaders, or *egwugwu*, also represent the nine villages of Umuofia. Okonkwo does not sit among the other eight leaders, or elders, while they listen to a dispute between an estranged husband and wife. The wife, Mgbafo, had been severely beaten by her husband. Her brother took her back to their family's village, but her husband wanted her back home. The egwugwu tell the husband to take wine to his in-laws and beg his wife to come home. One elder wonders why such a trivial dispute would come before the egwugwu.

In her role as priestess, Chielo tells Ekwefi (Okonkwo's second wife) that Agbala (the Oracle of the Hills and Caves) needs to see Ezinma. Although Okonkwo and Ekwefi protest, Chielo takes a terrified Ezinma on her back and forbids anyone to follow. Chielo carries Ezinma to all nine villages and then enters the Oracle's cave. Ekwefi follows secretly, in spite of Chielo's admonitions, and waits at the entrance of the Oracle. Okonkwo surprises Ekwefi by arriving at the cave, and he also waits with her. The next morning, Chielo takes Ezinma to Ekwefi's hut and puts her to bed.

When Ogbuefi Ezeudu dies, Okonkwo worries because the last time that Ezeudu visited him was when he warned Okonkwo against participating in the killing of Ikemefuna. Ezeudu was an important leader in the village and achieved three titles of the clan's four, a rare accomplishment. During the large funeral, Okonkwo's gun goes off, and Ezeudu's sixteen-year-old son is killed accidentally.

Because the accidental killing of a clansman is a crime against the earth goddess, Okonkwo and his family must be exiled from Umuofia for seven years. The family moves to Okonkwo's mother's native village, Mbanta. After they depart Umuofia, a group of village men destroy Okonkwo's compound and kill his animals to cleanse the village of Okonkwo's sin. Obierika stores Okonkwo's yams in his barn and wonders about the old traditions of the Igbo culture.

Okonkwo is welcomed to Mbanta by his maternal uncle, Uchendu, a village elder. He gives Okonkwo a plot of land on which to farm and build a compound for his family. But Okonkwo is depressed, and he blames his *chi* (or personal spirit) for his failure to achieve lasting greatness.

During Okonkwo's second year in exile, he receives a visit from his best friend, Obierika, who recounts sad news about the village of Abame: After a white man rode into the village on a bicycle, the elders of Abame consulted their Oracle, which told them that the white man would destroy their clan and other clans. Consequently, the villagers killed the white man. But weeks later, a large group of men slaughtered the villagers in retribution. The village of Abame is now deserted.

Okonkwo and Uchendu agree that the villagers were foolish to kill a man whom they knew nothing about. Later, Obierika gives Okonkwo money that he received from selling Okonkwo's yams and seed-yams, and he promises to do so until Okonkwo returns to Umuofia.

Six missionaries, including one white man, arrive in Mbanta. The white man speaks to the people about Christianity. Okonkwo believes that the man speaks nonsense, but his son, Nwoye, is captivated and becomes a convert of Christianity.

The Christian missionaries build a church on land given to them by the village leaders. However, the land is a part of the Evil Forest, and according to tradition, the villagers believe that the missionaries will die because they built their church on cursed land. But when nothing happens to the missionaries, the people of Mbanta conclude that the missionaries possess extraordinary power and magic. The first recruits of the missionaries are *efulefu*, the weak and worthless men of the village. Other villagers, including a woman, soon convert to Christianity. The missionaries then go to Umuofia and start a school. Nwoye leaves his father's hut and moves to Umuofia so he can attend the school.

Okonkwo's exile is over, so his family arranges to return to Umuofia. Before leaving Mbanta, they prepare a huge feast for Okonkwo's mother's kinsmen in appreciation of their gratitude during Okonkwo's seven years of exile.

When Okonkwo returns to Umuofia, he discovers that the village has changed during his absence. Many men have renounced their titles and have converted to Christianity. The white men have built a prison; they have established a government court of law, where people are tried for breaking the white man's laws; and they also employ natives of Umuofia.

Okonkwo wonders why the Umuofians have not incited violence to rid the village of the white man's church and oppressive government.

Some members of the Igbo clan like the changes in Umuofia. Mr. Brown, the white missionary, respects the Igbo traditions. He makes an effort to learn about the Igbo culture and becomes friendly with some of the clan leaders. He also encourages Igbo people of all ages to get an education. Mr. Brown tells Okonkwo that Nwoye, who has taken the name Isaac, is attending a teaching college. Nevertheless, Okonkwo is unhappy about the changes in Umuofia.

After Mr. Brown becomes ill and is forced to return to his homeland, Reverend James Smith becomes the new head of the Christian church. But Reverend Smith is nothing like Mr. Brown; he is intolerant of clan customs and is very strict.

Violence arises after Enoch, an overzealous convert to Christianity, unmasks an egwugwu. In retaliation, the egwugwu burn Enoch's compound and then destroy the Christian church because the missionaries have caused the Igbo people many problems.

When the District Commissioner returns to Umuofia, he learns about the destruction of the church and asks six leaders of the village, including Okonkwo, to meet with him. The men are jailed until they pay a fine of two hundred and fifty bags of cowries. The people of Umuofia collect the money and pay the fine, and the men are set free.

The next day at a meeting for clansmen, five court messengers who intend to stop the gathering approach the group. Suddenly, Okonkwo jumps forward and beheads the man in charge of the messengers with his machete. When none of the other clansmen attempt to stop the messengers who escape, Okonkwo realizes that they will never go to war and that Umuofia will surrender. Everything has fallen apart for Okonkwo; he commits suicide by hanging himself.

List of Characters

Okonkwo (Oh-*kawn*-kwoh)   The central character of *Things Fall Apart*. A young leader of the African Igbo community of Umuofia (Oo-moo-*oh*-fee-ah), he is known as a fierce warrior as well as a successful farmer. He is determined to overcome the stigma left by his father's laziness and wastefulness.

Unoka (Ooh-*no*-kah)   Okonkwo's father, known for his weakness and lack of responsibility.

Nwoye (Nuh-*woh*-yeh)   Okonkwo's oldest son, age twelve at the book's beginning. He is innately a sensitive young man.

Ikemefuna (Ee-keh-*meh*-foo-nah)   A boy of fourteen who is given to Umuofia by a neighboring village to avoid war. He is a clever, resourceful young man.

Ekwefi (Eh-*kweh*-fee)   Okonkwo's second wife; the mother of Ezinma, her only living child.

Ezinma (Eh-*zeen*-mah)   Daughter of Ekwefi and Okonkwo; Ekwefi's only surviving child.

Ojiubo (Oh-jee-*ooh*-boh)   Okonkwo's third wife; the mother of several of Okonkwo's children.

Obierika (Oh-bee-*air*-ee-kah)   Okonkwo's best friend, who often represents the voice of reason. He is the father of Maduka (son) and Ekueke (daughter).

Chielo (*Chee*-eh-loh)   A village widow who is also the priestess of Agbala.

Agbala (*Ahg*-bah-lah)   The Oracle of the Hills and the Caves, who influences all aspects of Umuofian life. She is based on the real Oracle at Awka, who controlled Igbo life for centuries.

Mr. Brown   The first white Christian missionary in Umuofia and Mbanta. An understanding and accommodating man, he is inclined to listen to the Igbos.

Mr. Kiaga (Kee-*ah*-gah)   The native interpreter for the missionaries. He is a teacher and a leader of the new church in Mbanta.

The Reverend James Smith   A strict, stereotypical white Christian missionary, he takes over the church after Mr. Brown's departure.

The District Commissioner A stern, stereotypical white colonial administrator of Umuofia. He follows regulations to the letter and possesses little knowledge or understanding of the people for whom he tries to administer a new government

Character Map

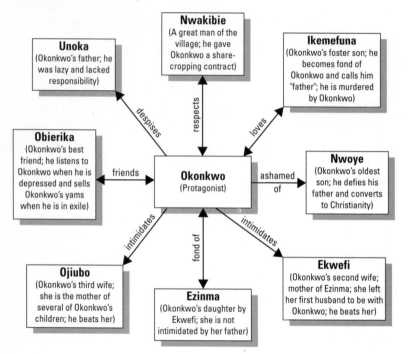

Nwakibie
(A great man of the village; he gave Okonkwo a share-cropping contract)

Unoka
(Okonkwo's father; he was lazy and lacked responsibility)

Ikemefuna
(Okonkwo's foster son; he becomes fond of Okonkwo and calls him "father"; he is murdered by Okonkwo)

Obierika
(Okonkwo's best friend; he listens to Okonkwo when he is depressed and sells Okonkwo's yams when he is in exile)

Okonkwo
(Protagonist)

Nwoye
(Okonkwo's oldest son; he defies his father and converts to Christianity)

Ojiubo
(Okonkwo's third wife; she is the mother of several of Okonkwo's children; he beats her)

Ezinma
(Okonkwo's daughter by Ekwefi; she is not intimidated by her father)

Ekwefi
(Okonkwo's second wife; mother of Ezinma; she left her first husband to be with Okonkwo; he beats her)

despises

respects

loves

friends

ashamed of

intimidates

fond of

intimidates

CRITICAL COMMENTARIES

The sections that follow provide great tools for supplementing your reading of *Things Fall Apart*. First, in order to enhance your understanding of and enjoyment from reading, we provide quick summaries in case you have difficulty when you read the original literary work. Each summary is followed by commentary: literary devices, character analyses, themes, and so on. Keep in mind that the interpretations here are solely those of the author of this study guide and are used to jumpstart your thinking about the work. No single interpretation of a complex work like *Things Fall Apart* is infallible or exhaustive, and you'll likely find that you interpret portions of the work differently from the author of this study guide. Read the original work and determine your own interpretations, referring to these Notes for supplemental meanings only.

Part One
Chapter 1

Summary

Set around the turn of the century, the novel focuses first on the hero of the book, Okonkwo, and on his late father, Unoka. Okonkwo is a respected leader within the Igbo (formerly spelled *Ibo*) community of Umuofia in eastern Nigeria. About twenty years ago, Okonkwo distinguished himself and brought honor to his village when he wrestled and threw to the ground Amalinze the Cat, a man who had not been defeated for seven years. Since then, Okonkwo's reputation as a wrestler has grown throughout the nine villages of Umuofia. He is known to be quickly angered, especially when dealing with unsuccessful men like his father, who died ten years ago deeply in debt.

Because of Unoka's laziness and wastefulness, the community had considered him a failure and laughingstock; he was a continual source of deep shame to Okonkwo. Even though he had a family to care for, Unoka frequently borrowed money and then squandered it on palm-wine and merrymaking with his neighbors, thus neglecting his family who barely had enough to eat.

The story is told about the day, years ago, when Unoka was visited by Okoye, a successful neighbor. After the traditional ceremonial courtesies and small talk, Okoye asked Unoka for the two hundred cowries that Unoka had borrowed two years earlier. Okoye needed the money for the ceremony in which he would purchase the third highest title of honor.

Unoka burst into laughter and pointed to the wall on which he recorded his debts. He told Okoye that tradition required him to repay his largest debts before repaying small ones like his debt to Okoye. Okoye left without his money.

Despite his father's shameful reputation, Okonkwo is now highly respected in Umuofia, which honors individual achievement rather than family heritage. Still a young man in his thirties, Okonkwo has become a wealthy farmer of yams—a sacred crop—and supports three wives, a significant indicator of wealth and "manliness." Furthermore, he is known for his incredible prowess in two intertribal wars, and he holds two honorific titles, though his father died with none.

Because Okonkwo is honored as one of the greatest men in his community, he will be asked to look after a young man who will be given as a peace offering to Umuofia by the neighboring village of Mbaino, which hopes to avoid war with Umuofia.

Commentary

Although not indicated in this chapter, the events of *Things Fall Apart* take place in the late 1800s and early 1900s, just before and during the early days of the British Empire's expansion in Nigeria. The novel depicts details about life in an African culture much different from Western culture. In this chapter, Achebe reveals the following aspects of Igbo culture:

- Legends and traditions (the fight with a spirit of the wild by the founder of their village)

- Symbols of honor (titles)

- Indicators of wealth (yams, cowries)

- Marriage customs (more than one wife)

- The reckoning of time (market, a week of four days)

- Social rituals (kola nuts, alligator pepper, chalk, small talk, and proverbs)

- Music, entertainment, food, and drink

In his goal to demonstrate the complexity and sophistication of Igbo society, Achebe gradually introduces these details when they are relevant to the story.

Character Insight

Chapter 1 describes Okonkwo's principal accomplishments that establish his important position in Igbo society. These details alone provide insight into Okonkwo's character and motivation. Driving himself toward tribal success and recognition, he is trying to bury the unending shame that he feels regarding the faults and failures of his late father, Unoka. Essentially, Okonkwo exhibits qualities of manhood in Igbo society.

Familiar with Western literature and its traditional forms, Achebe structures *Things Fall Apart* in the tradition of a Greek tragedy, with the story centered around Okonkwo, the tragic hero. Aristotle defined the *tragic hero* as a character who is superior and noble, one who demonstrates great courage and perseverance but is undone because of a tragic personal flaw in his character.

Theme

In this first chapter, Achebe sets up Okonkwo as a man much respected for his considerable achievements and noble virtues—key qualities of a tragic hero. Okonkwo's tragic flaw is his obsession with manliness; his fear of looking weak like his father drives him to commit irrational acts of violence that undermine his nobleness. In the chapters ahead, the reader should note the qualities and actions that begin to reveal the tragic flaw in Okonkwo's otherwise admirable actions, words, ideas, and relationships with others.

Literary Device

At the end of Chapter 1, Achebe foreshadows the presence of Ikemefuna in Okonkwo's household and also the teenage boy's ultimate fate by referring to him as a "doomed" and "ill-fated lad."

One of the most significant social markers of Igbo society is introduced in this chapter—its unique system of honorific titles. Throughout the book, titles are reference points by which members of Igbo society frequently compare themselves with one another (especially Okonkwo). These titles are not conferred by higher authorities, but they are acquired by the individual who can afford to pay for them. As a man accumulates wealth, he may gain additional recognition and prestige by "taking a title." He may also purchase titles for male members of his family (this aspect is revealed later). In the process of taking a title, the man pays significant initiation fees to the men who already hold the title.

A Umuofian man can take as many as four titles, each apparently more expensive than its predecessor. A man with sufficient money to pay the fee begins with the first level—the most common title—but many men cannot go beyond the first title. Each title taken may be shown by physical signs, such as an anklet or marks on the feet or face, so others can determine who qualifies for certain titles.

The initiation fees are so large that some writers have referred to the system as a means for "redistributing wealth." Some Native American tribes of the Pacific Northwest observe their own version of redistributing wealth through a *potlatch ceremony* at which the guests receive gifts from the person gaining the honor as a show of wealth for others to exceed.

Glossary

(Here and in the following chapters, difficult words and phrases, as well as allusions and historical references, are explained.)

gyre a circular or spiral motion; a revolution. The word appears in the book's opening quotation from a W.B. Yeats poem, "The Second Coming."

Okonkwo The name implies male pride and stubbornness.

Umuofia The community name, which means *children of the forest* and *a land undisturbed by European influences*.

harmattan a dry, dusty wind that blows from the Sahara in northern Africa toward the Atlantic, especially from November to March.

Unoka Okonkwo's father's name; its translation, *home is supreme*, implies a tendency to stay home and loaf instead of achieve fame and heroism.

cowries shells of the cowrie, a kind of mollusk related to snails and found in warm seas; especially the shells of the money cowrie, formerly used as currency in parts of Africa and southern Asia.

egwugwu leaders of the clan who wear masks during certain rituals and speak on behalf of the spirits; the term can be either singular or plural.

markets Igbo weeks are four days long, and the market day is on the first of day each week; therefore, three or four markets is a period of twelve to sixteen days.

kites birds of prey with long, pointed wings and, usually, a forked tail; they prey especially on insects, reptiles, and small mammals.

Okoye an everyman name comparable to John Doe in English. Okoye represents all the people to whom Unoka owes money.

kola nut the seed of the cola, an African tree. The seed contains caffeine and yields an extract; it represents vitality and is used as a courteous, welcoming snack, often with alligator pepper.

alligator pepper   a small brown fruit of an African shrub, whose hot seeds are like black pepper; also called *offe*. The seeds may be ground and blended with kola nut in the ritual welcome of visitors.

chalk   a material that represents peace. The Umuofians use chalk to signify personal honors and status by marking the floor and the toe or face, according to the level of honorific title they have taken. For example, Okoye marks his toe to indicate his first title.

Mbaino   This community name means *four settlements*.

ekwe   a drum.

udu   a clay pot.

ogene   a gong.

Ibo   a member of a people of southeastern Nigeria; known for their art and their skills as traders. Today, the word is spelled *Igbo* (the *g* is not pronounced).

Idemili title   This title, named after the river god Idemili, is the third-level title of honor in Umuofia.

Chapter 2

Summary

One night, as Okonkwo is settling on his bed, he hears the beat of a drum and the voice of the town crier. The messenger summons every man in Umuofia to gather at the marketplace the next morning. Okonkwo wonders whether the emergency concerns war with a neighboring clan. War does not frighten Okonkwo, because he knows that it frightened his cowardly father. In Umuofia's most recent war, for example, Okonkwo brought home his fifth human head.

The next morning, Okonkwo joins the men in the marketplace to hear the important message. A powerful orator shouts a welcome to them by greeting them in all four directions while punching his clenched fist into the air; the assembled men shout in response. After silence returns, he angrily tells the crowd that a Umuofian woman has been killed in Mbaino while she was attending the market. The outraged crowd finally agrees that Umuofia should follow its usual course of action: Give Mbaino a choice of either going to war with Umuofia or offering Umuofia a young man and a young virgin as compensation for the death of the Umuofian woman.

Umuofian's power in war and magic is feared by its neighbors, who know that Umuofia will not go to war without first trying to negotiate a peaceful settlement and seeking the acceptance of war by its Oracle. Everyone knows that a war with Mbaino would be a just war, so the clan sends Okonkwo as their emissary to negotiate with Mbaino; he returns two days later with a young man and a virgin offered by Mbaino.

The elders of Umuofia decide that the girl should live with the man whose wife was killed and that the young man, named Ikemefuna, belongs to the clan as a whole. They ask Okonkwo to take fourteen-year-old Ikemefuna into his home while the clan decides what to do with him. Okonkwo then gives the care of Ikemefuna to his senior wife, the mother of Nwoye, his oldest son, who is twelve. Ikemefuna is quite frightened, especially because he does not understand what has happened or why he is in Umuofia, separated from his family. The elders decide that the teenage boy will live in Okonkwo's household for three years.

Because Okonkwo is continually afraid that someone may consider him weak, he rules his household with a stern hand and a fierce voice, causing everyone to fear his explosive temper. When he was a child, a playmate called his father *agbala*, which means woman and also a man who has taken no title. Okonkwo learned to hate everything his father loved, including gentleness as well as idleness. He also sees signs of laziness in his son Nwoye. To purge himself of the reminder of his father, Okonkwo nags and beats Nwoye daily.

In his family compound, Okonkwo lives in a hut of his own, and each of his three wives lives in a hut of her own with her children. The prosperous compound also includes an enclosure with stacks of yams, sheds for goats and hens, and a medicine house, where Okonkwo keeps the symbols of his personal god and ancestral spirits and where he offers prayers for himself and his family. He works long hours on his farms and expects others to do the same. Although the members of his family do not possess his strength, they work without complaint.

Commentary

In Chapter 2, the reader begins to see beliefs and practices of the Igbo tradition that are particularly significant in the story—for example, the wide division between masculine and feminine actions and responsibilities. Respect and success are based on only manly activities and accomplishments; taking care of children and hens, on the other hand, are womanly activities.

In Okonkwo's determination to be a perfect example of manhood, he begins to reveal the consequences of his fear of weakness—his tragic flaw. Okonkwo hates not only idleness but also gentleness; he demands that his family works as long as he does (without regarding their lesser physical stamina), and he nags and beats his oldest son, Nwoye.

Achebe continues weaving traditional elements of Igbo society into Chapter 2. The marketplace gathering illustrates the Igbo society's reverence for what is "manly"—for example, the male villagers' loyalty to each other when they refer to the woman murdered by another village as "a daughter of Umuofia." This scene also illustrates the ceremonial nature of town meetings, as the speaker shouts the customary greeting to the crowd while turning in four different directions. In addition, the reader learns that Umuofian religious traditions include the worship of wooden objects representing not only one's personal god but also the ancestral spirits to whom one prays and makes sacrifices.

Achebe continues to use the art of traditional storytelling and references to legends and sayings of the time to illustrate what people believe and respect. For example:

■ Okonkwo remembers from childhood when his father was called a woman.

■ The proverb, "When the moon is shining, the cripple becomes hungry for a walk," represents a belief in the protective quality of moonlight in contrast with the fear of the darkness.

■ The legend of the old woman with one leg explains, in part, why the other clans fear Umuofia.

Glossary

Ogbuefi   a person with a high title, as in Ogbuefi Ezeugo (the orator) and Ogbuefi Udo (the man whose wife was killed in Mbaino).

Ezeugo   the name for a person of high religious significance, such as an Igbo priest.

Udo   peace.

about ten thousand men   The nine villages of Umuofia unlikely have as many as ten thousand men. This saying probably means every man of the community—an example of *hyperbole*, an exaggeration not intended to be taken literally.

Umuofia kwenu   a shout of approval and greeting that means *United Umuofia!*

agadi-nwayi   an old woman.

Oracle   the place where, or medium by which, the deities are consulted; here, the Oracle of the Hills and the Caves.

a just war   Societies throughout history have rationalized certain wars as justified for religious or cultural reasons. For example, in the fifth century, St. Augustine of the early Christian church wrote extensively about the just war; the Crusades of the late Middle Ages were initiated as holy wars; and today's Muslim word *jihad* means holy war.

emissary   a person or agent sent on a specific mission.

ndichie   elders.

obi   a hut within a compound.

compound   an enclosed space with a building or group of buildings within it.

Chapter 3

Summary

Chapter 3 describes incidents from Okonkwo's childhood and young adulthood—incidents that have contributed to Okonkwo's flawed character.

According to the first story from Okonkwo's past, his father, Unoka, consulted the Oracle of the Hills and Caves, asking why he had produced bad harvests each year in spite of his sacrifices and planting procedures. During his story, Chika (the priestess of the Oracle) interrupted him angrily and told him that he hadn't offended the gods, but in his laziness, he took the easy way out by planting on exhausted land. She told him to go home and "work like a man."

Bad fortune followed Unoka, even to his death. He died of swelling in his stomach and limbs—an affliction not acceptable to Ani, the earth goddess. He therefore could not be buried properly, so he was taken to the Evil Forest to rot, making Okonkwo even more ashamed of his father.

In the second story from Okonkwo's past, the young Okonkwo was preparing to plant his first farm in yams—a man's crop—while his mother and sisters grew women's crops—such things as coco-yams and cassava. Because Okonkwo had received nothing from his father, he began his farming through share-cropping. To get help for his planting, he visited Nwakibie, a great man of the village, symbolized by his three barns, nine wives, and thirty children. After the proper greetings and rituals, Okonkwo asked Nwakibie for seed-yams and pledges his hard work in growing and harvesting them. According to the share-cropping contract, Okonkwo would return two-thirds of what he grew to Nwakibie and receive only a third of the total crop for himself, his parents, and his sisters. Nwakibie had already turned down similar requests from other young men. But he acknowledged Okonkwo's earnestness and ambition and gave Okonkwo twice the number of seed-yams he'd hoped for.

The growing season that followed was disastrous for Okonkwo as well as for most other farmers of the village. The land suffered first a great drought and then unending rain and floods—a combination ruinous to the season's harvest. Okonkwo was deeply discouraged, but he knew that he would survive because of his determination to succeed.

Commentary

Literary Device

Achebe's use of storytelling further illustrates how Okonkwo's resentment of his father grew, as well as how his own determination to succeed was tested—the two sides of his characterization as tragic hero.

The separation between the man's world and the woman's world in Umuofian culture is again emphasized in this chapter—first, in the roles of the women in the ritual wine-drinking and, later, in the classification of crops. Coco-yams, beans, and cassava are considered women's crops; in contrast, the yam is identified as the "king of crops"—a man's crop.

Chapter 3 also illustrates several traditional ideas and truths that shape day-to-day Igbo life. These principles are often expressed through indirect language and symbols in the following proverbs:

- "A toad does not run in the daytime for nothing."

- "The lizard that jumped from the high iroko tree to the ground said that he would praise himself if no one else did."

- "[Because] men have learned to shoot without missing, [Eneke the bird] has learned to fly without perching."

- "You can tell a ripe corn by its look."

These traditional expressions demonstrate the great respect and courtesy that the Igbo people show to one another because the speaker uses veiled language when making comments about himself (Okonkwo in the lizard example, and Nwakibie in the Eneke example); about others (Ogbuefi Idigo talking about Obiako in the toad example); about the person he is addressing (Nwakibie speaking to Okonkwo in the corn example); and about life in general even to oneself (Okonkwo in the old woman example). This symbolic language represents a high level of cultural sensitivity and sophistication.

An especially significant concept introduced in this chapter is the belief in personal *chi*. At its simplest level, chi parallels the Western concept of soul, although chi is a more complex idea. The Igbo believe that an individual's fate and abilities for the coming life are assigned to the chi, and each individual is given a chi by the Creator (Chukwu) at the moment of conception. Before each reincarnation, the individual bargains for improved circumstances in the next life. The chi thus becomes one's personal god that guides one to fulfill the expected destiny. On the one hand, the individual is ruled by his chi, but on the other hand, only the individual can make the most of the fate planned through the chi.

Notice that Achebe's first name, Chinua, begins with chi. Achebe explained the usage of chi in the following excerpt: "When we talk about chi, we're talking about the individual spirit, and so you find the word in all kinds of combinations. Chinwe, which is my wife's name, means *chi owns me*; mine is Chinua, which is a shortened form of an expression that means *may a chi fight for me*. My son is named Chidi, which means *chi is there*. So it's [in] almost [all my family members' names] in one form or the other. Our youngest girl asked me why she didn't have chi in her name. She thought it was some kind of discrimination, so she took the name Chioma, which means *good chi*."

Glossary

Agbala, the Oracle   the prophet of the Igbo. Achebe bases the Agbala Oracle (the Oracle of the Hills and the Caves) on the Awka Oracle that was destroyed by the British. Chielo was the priestess who spoke to Unoka on behalf of the god Agbala.

Ani   the earth goddess who owns all land.

chi   a significant cultural concept and belief meaning one's personal deity; also one's destiny or fate.

Nna-ayi   translated as *our father*; a greeting of respect.

sharecropping   working land for a share of the crop, especially as a tenant farmer. Here, Okonkwo works as a sharecropper to obtain seed-yams.

coco-yam   the edible, spherical-shaped tuber of the taro plant grown in the tropics and eaten like potatoes or ground into flour, cooked to a paste, or fermented for beer. Here, the round coco-yam (a woman's crop) is a different tuber than the elongated-shaped yam (a man's crop).

cassava any of several plants (genus *Manihot* and especially *M. esculenta*) of the spurge family grown in the tropics for their fleshy, edible rootsticks that produce a nutritious starch. Here, the plant also provides valuable leaves for livestock feed as well as tubers, which are prepared like coco-yams.

Chapter 4

Summary

In spite of Okonkwo's beginnings in poverty and misfortune, he has risen as one of the most respected elders of the clan. Yet others remark on how harshly he deals with men less successful than himself. For example, at a meeting to discuss the next ancestral feast, Osugo—a man without titles—contradicts Okonkwo, who in turn insults Osugo by declaring the meeting is "for men." When others at the meeting side with Osugo, Okonkwo apologizes.

Okonkwo's hard-earned success is evident because the clan chooses Okonkwo to carry the war ultimatum to their enemy, the enemy treats him with great respect in the negotiations, and the elders select Okonkwo to care for Ikemefuna until they decide what to do with him. Once the young man is entrusted to Okonkwo's care, the rest of the clan forgets him for three years.

At first, Ikemefuna is very unhappy—he misses his mother and sister, he tries to run away, and he won't eat. After Okonkwo threatens to beat him, Ikemefuna finally eats, but then vomits and becomes ill for twelve days. As he recovers, he seems to lose his fear and sadness.

Ikemefuna has become very popular in Okonkwo's house, especially with Nwoye and the other children. To them, he seems to know everything and can make useful things like flutes, rodent traps, and bows. Even Okonkwo has inwardly become fond of Ikemefuna, but he does not show affection—a womanly sign of weakness. He treats Ikemefuna with a heavy hand, as he does other members of his family, although he allows Ikemefuna to accompany him like a son to meetings and feasts, carrying his stool and his bag. Ikemefuna calls Okonkwo "father."

During the annual Week of Peace just before planting time, tradition permits no one in the village to speak a harsh word to another person. One day during this week, Okonkwo's youngest wife, Ojiugo, goes to a friend's house to braid her hair, and she forgets to prepare Okonkwo's afternoon meal and feed her children. When Ojiugo returns, Okonkwo beats her severely. Even when he is reminded of the ban on violence, he doesn't stop the beating. Because Okonkwo's violation of peace can jeopardize the whole village's crops, the priest of the earth goddess orders Okonkwo to make offerings at his shrine. Although Okonkwo inwardly regrets his "great evil," he never admits to an error. His offensive breaking of the peace and the priest's mild punishment are talked about in the village.

After the sacred week, the farmers of the village begin to plant their harvest. Okonkwo allows Ikemefuna and Nwoye to help him collect, count, and prepare the seed-yams for planting, though he continually finds fault with their efforts. He believes that he is simply helping them learn the difficult and manly art of seed-yam preparation.

Soon, the rainy season begins and the planting takes place, followed by the intense period of care for the young plants. During the resting time between planting and harvest, the friendship between Ikemefuna and Nwoye grows even stronger.

Commentary

To secure his manliness, Okonkwo believes that he should beat members of his family (Nwoye, Ikemefuna, Ojiugo, and his wives) and that he should ridicule men who remind him of his father—even for slight annoyances. Although he may inwardly experience emotions of affection and regret, he cannot show these emotions to others, so he isolates himself through extreme actions.

Two more examples of traditional wisdom are used when talking about Okonkwo:

- **"Those whose palm-kernels were cracked for them by a benevolent spirit should not forget to be humble."** This proverb means that a man whose success is a result of luck must not forget that he has faults. Okonkwo, however, had "cracked them himself," because he overcame poverty not through luck, but through hard work and determination.

- **"When a man says yes, his chi says yes also."** This Igbo proberb implies that a man's actions affect his destiny as determined by his chi. Okonkwo's chi is considered "good," but he "[says] yes very strongly, so his chi [agrees]." In other words, Okonkwo's actions to overcome adversity seem justified, but because he is guided by his chi, his denial of kindness, gentleness, and affection for less successful men will prove self-destructive. (The chi itself is somewhat ambiguous. Review the discussion of chi in the Commentary for Chapter 3.)

The end of the chapter refers to Ikemefuna's favorite story about "the ant [who] holds his court in splendor and the sands dance forever." Watch for this story to reappear under tragic circumstances.

Glossary

Osugo   The name means a low-ranked person.

Week of Peace   In Umofia, a sacred week in which violence is prohibited.

nza   a small but aggressive bird.

nso-ani   a sin against the earth goddess, Ani.

Amadiora   the god of thunder and lightning.

Chapter 5

Summary

The village of Umuofia prepares for the Feast of the New Yam, which takes place just before the harvest. All yams left over from the old year must be thrown away, and everything used in preparing, cooking, and serving yams must be thoroughly washed before being used for the new crop. Relatives and other guests are invited from afar for the feast; Okonkwo invites his wives' relatives. While everyone else seems enthusiastic about the coming festival, Okonkwo knows that he will grow tired of celebrating the festival for days; he would rather tend to his farm.

Near the end of the preparations, Okonkwo's suppressed anger and resentment about the feast explodes when he thinks someone has killed one of his banana trees. However, leaves have merely been cut off from the tree to wrap food. When his second wife, Ekwefi, admits to taking the leaves, Okonkwo beats her severely to release his pent-up anger. Then he sends for his rusty gun to go hunting—Okonkwo is not a hunter nor is he skilled with a gun. When Ekwefi mumbles about "guns that never shot," he grabs his gun, aims it at her, and pulls the trigger. Although it goes off, she is not injured. Okonkwo sighs and walks away with the gun.

Despite Okonkwo's outbursts, the festival is celebrated with great joy, even in his household and by Ekwefi after her beating and near shooting. Like most people of the village, she looks forward to the second day of the feast and its great wrestling matches between men of the village and men of neighboring villages. This contest is the same kind in which Okonkwo, years earlier, not only won the wrestling match but also won Ekwefi's heart.

Okonkwo's wives and daughters excitedly prepare the yams for the feast in anticipation of the contest. As his evening meal is served by daughters of each of his wives, Okonkwo acknowledges to himself how especially fond he is of his daughter Ezinma. As if to offset his soft feelings, however, he scolds her twice while she sits waiting for him to eat.

Commentary

Chapter 4 repeatedly illustrates Okonkwo's volatility—his readiness to explode into violence at slight provocations. His feelings often differ from what he says or does. Although the people of the village respect him and his accomplishments, he does not quite fit in with his peers, some of whom disagree with his treatment of less successful men.

Okonkwo does not even enjoy the leisurely ceremonial feast as others do. His impatience with the festivities is so great that he erupts. He falsely accuses one of his wives, beats her, and then makes an apparent attempt to shoot her. Further evidence of his violent nature is revealed when he moves his feet in response to the drums of the wrestling dance and trembles "with the desire to conquer and subdue . . . like the desire for a woman." Okonkwo's need to express anger through violence is clearly a fatal flaw in his character. His stubborn and often irrational behavior is beginning to set him apart from the rest of the village.

In contrast, Okonkwo exhibits feelings of love and affection—his first encounter with Ekwefi and his fondness for Ezinma, his daughter. However, Okonkwo considers such emotions signs of weakness that betray his manliness, so he hides his feelings and acts harshly to conceal them.

The amount of detail included about the Feast of the New Yam, just before the annual harvest, underscores how closely the life of the community relates to the production of its food. The description of household preparations for the festival reveals two significant issues about Igbo culture:

■ The roles of women and daughters to keep the household running smoothly and to prepare for special occasions even though they can hold positions of leadership in the village.

■ The insignificant impact a wife beating and a near shooting have on family life, as if violence is an acceptable part of day-to-day life in the household.

For the first time in the story, Achebe mentions guns. Because of an outgrowth of Igbo trade with the rest of the world, Western technology actually arrived in the village before the Westerners did. Umuofia was not a completely isolated community.

Glossary

calabash   the dried, hollow shell of a gourd, used as a bowl, cup, and so on.

yam foo-foo   pounded and mashed yam pulp.

cam wood   a dye from a West African redwood tree that is used by women to redden their skins before decorating themselves with other patterns for special occasions.

bride-price   in some cultures, money and property given to a prospective bride's family by the prospective groom and his family.

Ezinma   Ekwefi and Okonkwo's daughter; meaning true beauty. She is also called Nma and Ezigbo, which mean the good one (child).

ilo   the village gathering place and playing field; an area for large celebrations and special events.

making inyanga   flaunting or showing off.

Chapter 6

Summary

On the second day of the festival, everyone gathers at the village playing field to watch the wrestling contest between men of the village and men of a neighboring village. The first matches, between two teams of boys fifteen or sixteen years old, provide entertainment and excitement before the main events. One of the victorious boys is Maduka, the son of Okonkwo's good friend Obierika. Neighbors greet each other and tension builds until matches between the real wrestlers begin.

The current priestess of the Oracle, Chielo, talks casually with Ekwefi about Okonkwo's attack on her and about Ekwefi's daughter Ezinma, of whom Chielo seems particularly fond.

As the drums thunder, two teams of twelve men challenge each other. Many expect the final match between the two greatest fighters in the villages to be uneventful because of the similar styles of the two wrestlers. However, the spectators are thrilled when the local fighter, Okafo, takes advantage of one of his opponent's moves and suddenly defeats him. The crowd carries the victorious Okafo on their shoulders with pride.

Commentary

The spectacle of the wrestling matches illustrates the value that is placed on physical agility and strength in the Igbo culture. In ways similar to today's sports, the wrestling events—even in their violence—provide vicarious pleasure for the spectators who consider the victors heroes and often carry them on their shoulders. Many years earlier, Okonkwo himself sparked his reputation as a powerful man by defeating an opponent who had wrestled undefeated for seven years.

This scene also displays the sense of community and kinship among members of the village, as in the brief exchange between Ekwefi and her neighbor Chielo, the priestess of the Oracle Agbala.

The conversation between Ekwefi and Chielo that begins with Chielo stating "And how is my daughter Ezinma?" includes several puzzling references to Ezinma. Except for the marketplace and gatherings such as the Feast of the New Yam, the women get little opportunity to visit other villagers who are not in their family. However, note the concern that Ekwefi has for Ezinma, as well as the Chielo's particular fondness for Ezinma, whom she calls "daughter." This scene implies that Chielo, the priestess, perhaps knows more about Ezinma's fate than she is revealing.

Glossary

silk-cotton tree   any of several large, tropical, trees (genera *Bombax* and *Ceiba*) of the bombax family that have capsular fruits with silky hairs around the seeds. Here, the tree is revered because it contains spirits of good children as yet unborn.

palm fronds   leaves of a palm tree. Here, they are tied together in clusters for "beating the ground" or the legs and feet of the pushing crowd.

Chielo   the name of the current priestess of Agbala, the Oracle of the Hills and the Caves.

Chapter 7

Summary

Nwoye and Ikemefuna spend all their time together like brothers. In the evenings, they sit with Okonkwo in his hut and listen to his manly stories of violence and bloodshed. Nwoye still enjoys his mother's folk tales and legends, but he tries to impress Okonkwo by acting masculine by pretending to dislike the women's stories and by grumbling about women. Okonkwo is inwardly pleased as Nwoye grows more tough and manly, and he credits the change to Ikemefuna's good influence.

One day while Okonkwo and his sons are working on the walls of the compound, a great black cloud descends upon the town. The villagers are joyful because they recognize the coming of the locusts, a great delicacy in Umuofia. Everyone sets out to catch them for roasting, drying, and eating.

As Okonkwo, Nwoye, and Ikemefuna are happily eating the rare food, Ogbuefi Ezeudu, the oldest man of the village, calls on Okonkwo to speak to him privately. He tells Okonkwo that the Oracle has decreed that Ikemefuna must be killed as part of the retribution for the woman killed three years before in Mbaino. He tells Okonkwo to take no part in the killing since the boy calls him "father."

Later, Okonkwo tells Ikemefuna that he is going home to Mbaino, but the boy does not believe him. When Nwoye hears that his friend is leaving, he bursts into tears and is beaten by his father.

Many men of Umuofia accompany Ikemefuna to the outskirts of the village and into the forest. With Okonkwo walking near him, Ikemefuna loses his fear and thinks about his family in Mbaino. Suddenly, Okonkwo drops to the rear of the group and Ikemefuna is afraid again. As the boy's back is turned, one of the men strikes the first blow with his machete. Ikemefuna cries out to Okonkwo, "My father, they have killed me!" and runs toward Okonkwo. Afraid to appear weak, Okonkwo kills Ikemefuna with his machete.

When Nwoye learns that Ikemefuna is dead, something changes within him. He recalls the feeling that he experienced one day when he heard a baby crying in the forest—a tragic reminder to him of the custom of leaving twins in the forest to die.

Commentary

Literary Device

With the killing of Ikemefuna, Achebe creates a devastating scene that evokes compassion for the young man and foreshadows the fall of Okonkwo, again in the tradition of the tragic hero. Along the way, the author sets up several scenes that juxtapose with the death scene:

- The opening scene of the chapter shows the increasing affection and admiration Okonkwo feels for Ikemefuna, as well as for Nwoye.

- On the journey with Ikemefuna and the other men of Umuofia, they hear the "peaceful dance from a distant clan."

In Chapter 2, the author comments that the fate of Ikemefuna is a "sad story" that is "still told in Umuofia unto this day." This observation suggests that the decision to kill Ikemefuna was not a customary one. Before dying, Ikemefuna thinks of Okonkwo as his "real father" and of what he wants to tell his mother, especially about Okonkwo. These elements combined suggest that the murder of Ikemefuna is senseless, even if the killing is in accordance with the Oracle and village decisions.

The murder scene is a turning point in the novel. Okonkwo participates in the ceremony for sacrificing the boy after being strongly discouraged, and he delivers the death blow because he is "afraid of being thought weak." At a deep, emotional level, Okonkwo kills a boy who "could hardly imagine that Okonkwo was not his real father"—someone whom Okonkwo truly loves as a son. Okonkwo has not only outwardly disregarded his people and their traditions, but he has also disregarded his inner feelings of love and protectiveness. This deep abyss between Okonkwo's divided selves accounts for the beginning of his decline.

For the first time in the novel, Okonkwo's son, Nwoye, emerges as a major character who, in contrast to his father, questions the long-standing customs of the clan. Achebe begins to show the boy's conflicting emotions; he is torn between being a fiercely masculine and physically strong person to please his father and allowing himself to cherish values and feelings that Okonkwo considers feminine and weak.

Glossary

eneke-nti-oba   bird that flies endlessly.

entrails   the inner organs of humans or animals; specifically, the intestines; viscera; guts.

tie-tie   a vine used like a rope; from Pidgin English *to tie*.

harbingers   persons or things that come before to announce or give an indication of what follows; heralds.

pestle   a tool, usually club-shaped, used to pound or grind substances in a mortar, or very hard bowl.

ozo   a class of men holding an ozo title; it also refers to the ritual which accompanies the granting of a title to a person.

Eze elina, elina   a favorite song of Ikemefuna's about how Danda the ant holds court and how the sand dances forever; it was introduced as a story at the end of Chapter 4.

twins   two born at the same birth. Here, according to Igbo custom, twins are considered evil and must be placed in earthenware pots and left to die in the forest.

Chapter 8

Summary

For two days after Ikemefuna's death, Okonkwo cannot eat or sleep; his thoughts return again and again to the boy who was like a son to him. On the third day, when his favorite daughter Ezinma brings him the food he finally requested, he wishes to himself that she was a boy. He wonders with disgust how a man with his battle record can react like a woman over the death of a boy.

Okonkwo visits his friend Obierika, hoping to escape thoughts of Ikemefuna. He praises Obierika's son Maduka for his victory in the wrestling match and complains about his own son's wrestling skills and mentally likens him to his own weak father, Unoka. To counter these thoughts with a manly deed of his own, Okonkwo asks his friend why he didn't join the other men in the sacrifice of Ikemefuna. Obierika replies that he "had something better to do." He expresses his disapproval of Okonkwo's role in killing Ikemefuna. The act, he says, will upset the Earth, and the earth goddess will get her revenge.

A man interrupts them to relay the news of the death of an elder of a neighboring village, a former Umuofia leader. His wife, also later on the same day, complicates the announcement of the elder's death and funeral. The mourners recalled that they "had one mind" and that he could do nothing without telling her. Okonkwo and Obierika disapprove of this lack of manly quality. They also discuss with regret the loss of prestige of the *ozo* title. Feeling renewed by the conversation, Okonkwo goes home and returns later to take part in a discussion of the bride-price with the suitor of Obierika's daughter. After the preliminaries, the bride-price is decided using a ritual. Her price is negotiated between the bride's family and the groom's relatives by passing back and forth quantities of sticks that represent numbers.

The men eat and drink for the rest of the evening while ridiculing the customs of the neighboring villages compared to their own. They also refer contemptuously to "white men," comparing their white skin to lepers' white skin.

Commentary

In the scenes of Chapter 8, the reader can begin to see Okonkwo's growing separation from his family members as well as from his from peers in the village. Okonkwo asks Nwoye to sit with him in his hut, seeking affirmation that he has done nothing wrong by killing Ikemefuna. But his son pulls away from him.

Even Okonkwo's friend, Obierika, disapproves of his role in the killing of Ikemefuna. Obierika is presented as a moderate, balanced man and thus serves as a contrast to Okonkwo. Obierika periodically questions tribal law and believes that some changes can improve their society. Okonkwo tends to cling to tradition regardless of the cost, as the killing of Ikemefuna illustrates. Essentially, Obierika is a man of thought and questioning, while Okonkwo is a man of action without questioning.

However, both men seem to agree that manliness does not allow a man and his wife to be inseparable and outwardly loving to each other. (A village woman who has died before her husband's death can be publicly announced, but a wife's death soon after her husband's may be a sign that she is guilty of killing him.) The couple is known to be almost inseparable in their day-to-day life—a sign of weakness in the husband, according to Okonkwo and Obierika. The village must wait until she is buried before they can officially announce the death of the man who was once a great warrior.

An example of the economic customs of the village is the marriage negotiations for Obierika's daughter. The opening ceremonies—the costume and jewelry of the bride, the use of the sticks, and the drinking of the palm-wine—illustrate the complexity of Umuofian ritual. These African customs are reminiscent of marriage customs in other cultures in which the bride's parents pay a dowry or pay the cost of the wedding (although in Igbo custom, the groom himself pays the bride-price). Such customs refute commonly held notions about primitive and uncivilized African society.

The first shadow of "the white man" appears in community conversation, revealing their lack of contact with white men and their aversion to them (similar to their aversion to lepers).

Glossary

plantain   a hybrid banana plant that is widely cultivated in the Western Hemisphere.

taboo   any social prohibition or restriction that results from convention or tradition.

uli   a liquid made from seeds that make the skin pucker; used for temporary tattoo-like decorations.

jigida   strings of hundreds of tiny beads worn snugly around the waist.

And these white men, they say, have no toes   The white men's toes are hidden because they are wearing shoes.

leprosy   a progressive infectious disease caused by a bacterium that attacks the skin, flesh, nerves, and so on; it is characterized by nodules, ulcers, white scaly scabs, deformities, and the eventual loss of sensation, and is apparently communicated only after long and close contact.

Chapter 9

Summary

Okonkwo finally enjoys a good night's sleep since the death of Ikemefuna, when suddenly, he is awakened by a banging at his door. His wife Ekwefi tells him that Ezinma is dying. Ekwefi's only living child, Ezinma is the light of her life; her nine other children have died in infancy. Ezinma is also a favorite of Okonkwo, and because of her spirit and cleverness, he sometimes wishes that she had been born a boy. Now she lies suffering with fever while Okonkwo gathers leaves, grasses, and barks for medicine.

Ezinma has survived many periods of illness in her life, and people have considered her an evil *ogbanje*, a child who dies young because she is possessed by an evil spirit that reenters the mother's womb to be born again. But she has lived much longer than Ekwefi's other children, and Ekwefi believes faith will bring the girl a long and happy life. A year ago, she was reassured when a medicine man dug up Ezinma's *iyi-uwa*, an object buried by ogbanje children. After Ezinma led the medicine man to the exact spot, he dug a deep pit in which he finally found a shiny pebble wrapped in a rag. Ezinma agreed that it was hers. The unearthing of the iyi-uwa was thought to break Ezinma's connection with the ogbanje world, and everyone believed that she would never become sick again.

At last, Okonkwo returns from the forest and prepares the medicine for his daughter, who inhales the fumes from a steaming pot and soon sleeps again.

Commentary

Just when Okonkwo's guilt over killing Ikemefuna seems to lessen, his rarely displayed devotion to his family is again tested. When Ekwefi informs him of his daughter's illness, he rushes out in the middle of the night to hunt for medicine in the woods. By nature, Okonkwo is not a cold and heartless man; he simply cannot escape the haunting images of his despised father's womanly qualities.

Ekwefi's dedication to her daughter Ezinma exemplifies the important role children play in a woman's life in Umuofian society. Ekwefi says that children are a "woman's crowning glory," and before Ezinma was born, her own life was consumed with the desire to have a healthy child. But nine times, she lost children in infancy. A woman's status in Igbo society is related to how many children she bears and how many of them are male.

But although women's child-bearing abilities are an important aspect of their status, Okonkwo and Ekwefi's deep concern and fondness for Ezinma shows that, despite the divide between manly and womanly qualities, woman play an essential role in Igbo society. Women are responsible for preparing most of the celebratory activities, which strengthen relations within the village and with other communities. Women also create the decorations for the huts as well as elaborate body art.

Another important aspect of women in Igbo society is represented by Chielo, who is significant because, as a woman, she speaks on behalf of the God Agbala. Chielo refers to Ezinma as her "daughter," which may indicate that she will replace Chielo's position as priestess.

In Chapter 6, Ekwefi was hopeful that Ezinma had "come to stay." This observation foreshadowed that Ezinma was no longer an ogbanje because the medicine man dug up her iyi-uwa.

Glossary

iba   fever, probably related to malaria.

ogbanje   a child possessed by an evil spirit that leaves the child's body upon death only to enter into the mother's womb to be reborn again within the next child's body.

iyi-uwa   a special stone linking an ogbanje child and the spirit world; The ogbanje is protected as long as the stone is not discovered and destroyed.

Chapter 10

Summary

Chapter 10 is devoted to a detailed description of a village public trial. At a gathering on the large village commons, the elders sit waiting on their stools while the other men crowd behind them. The women stand around the edges, looking on. A row of nine stools awaits the appearance of the nine *egwugwu*, who represent the spirits of their ancestors. Two small clusters of people stand at a respectful distance facing the elders and the empty stools. The opposing sides of a family dispute, the two groups wait for a hearing by the masked and costumed egwugwu, who finally appear from their nearby house with great fanfare and ceremony. As the egwugwu approach the stools, Okonkwo's wives notice that the second egwugwu walks with the springy step of Okonkwo and also that Okonkwo is not seated among the elders, but of course, they say nothing about this odd coincidence.

The egwugwu hear the case of Uzowulu, who claims that his in-laws took his wife Mgbafo from his house, and therefore, they should return her bride-price to him. Odukwe, Mgbafo's brother, does not deny Uzowulu's charges. He claims that his family took Mgbafo to rescue her from daily brutal beatings by Uzowulu, and he says that she will return to her husband only if he swears never to beat her again.

After the egwugwu retire to consult with each other, their leader, Evil Forest, returns a verdict: He orders Uzowulu to take wine to his in-laws and beg his wife to come back home with him. Evil Forest also reminds the husband that fighting with a woman is not brave. Evil Forest then instructs Odukwe to accept his brother-in-law's offer and let Mgbafo return to her husband. After the matter is settled, one village elder expresses wonder at why such an insignificant dispute would come before the egwugwu. Another elder reminds him that Uzowulu does not accept any decision unless it comes from the egwugwu.

Another case waits to be heard—one involving property.

Commentary

The author provides a close-up view of the community judicial system with its similarities to Western traditions. In the trial of Uzowulu versus his wife's family, both sides present their cases to the ruling members of society, the egwugwu. The nine egwugwu represent the nine villages of Umuofia, and each village has one egwugwu as its spokesperson. Okonkwo has obviously risen to a lofty position of village leadership if he has indeed been selected as the egwugwu representative for his village.

The egwugwu has similarities to a jury led by a foreman or judge. For example, after retiring to the jury room for deliberation with the other eight egwugwu, the foreman/judge returns a verdict that must be carried out. The public is allowed to watch the proceedings within the boundaries of their social groups—that is, the elders, other men, and women.

The subject of the dispute, domestic violence, is a familiar one today, but the way in which the community views Uzowulu beating his wife is not. The verdict illustrates the widespread disregard for women's rights by Umuofian men. After hearing the case, the egwugwu order Mgbafo to go back to Uzowulu if he begs her; they remind Uzowulu that fighting with a woman is not manly. The embarrassment of begging his wife is the only punishment Uzowulu receives. This case illustrates that, in Umuofian culture, a woman is the property of her husband, but unwarranted and excessive violence against her is, in theory, inappropriate. Note that one man among the spectators asks why such a "trifle [as wife beating] should come before the egwugwu."

The trial and its verdict also recall Okonkwo's treatment of his own wives and how quickly such treatment is forgotten.

Glossary

Aru oyim de de de dei! egwugwu language translated as *greetings to the physical body of a friend*. The egwugwu speak in a formal language that is difficult for the the Umuofians to understand. Each of the nine egwugwu represents a village of the Umuofian community. Together, the egwugwu form a tribunal to judge disputes.

Evil Forest   the name of the leader of the egwugwu; also the name of the forest where taboo objects and people are abandoned.

I am Dry-meat-that fills-the-mouth / I am Fire-that-burns-without-faggots   two phrases suggesting that Evil Forest is all-powerful. Faggots are bundles of sticks for burning.

Chapter 11

Summary

As Okonkwo relaxes in his hut after the evening meal, he listens to the voices of his wives and children telling folk stories. Ekwefi relates to Ezinma the tale of Tortoise, which explains why the Tortoise shell is not smooth. Just as it becomes Ezinma's turn to tell Ekwefi a story, they all hear the high-pitched wail of Chielo, the priestess of Agbala. She then comes to Okonkwo's hut and tells him that Agbala needs to see his daughter Ezinma. He begs her to let the child sleep and return in the morning, but Chielo does not listen and proceeds to Ekwefi's hut to find Ezinma.

Terrified of the priestess, Ezinma cries in fear, but she is forced to go with Chielo to Agbala's house in the sacred cave and hangs onto Chielo's back. As Ekwefi watches her only daughter leave, she decides to follow her.

Following Chielo's chanting voice, Ekwefi runs through the forest in the dark. She finally catches up with them but keeps out of sight. The priestess, however, senses that someone is following her and curses her pursuer. Ekwefi lets Chielo get farther ahead and soon realizes that they have passed Agbala's cave. They are heading toward Umuachi, the farthest village. But when they reach the village commons, Chielo turns around and begins to return the way she came, eventually moving toward the cave of Agbala.

Chielo and Ezinma disappear into the cave, and Ekwefi waits outside doubting that she can help her daughter if any harm comes to her. Suddenly, Ekwefi hears a noise behind her and turns to see a man standing with a machete in his hand. Okonkwo has come to take her place outside the cave, but she refuses to leave. She stays with him, grateful for his presence and concern. His strong, silent presence reminds Ekwefi of how she ran away from her first husband to be the wife of Okonkwo.

Commentary

The oral tradition of storytelling in Igbo culture is a means for teaching history and customs, for passing on legends and beliefs, and for explaining the natural as well as the supernatural worlds. The tradition is particularly well-illustrated in the long story about Tortoise and his shell. The story explains why a tortoise shell is not smooth, but it also reveals the proverb, "a man who makes trouble for others is also making it for himself"—another indication that Okonkwo is bringing misfortune upon himself.

In this chapter, Achebe presents a situation in which Okonkwo and Ekwefi consider their family more important than the customs of their people or even their own personal safety. Despite Chielo's warning about the Oracle Agbala, "Beware, woman, lest he strike you in his anger," Ekwefi risks her life for the sake of her daughter when she chooses to follow Chielo through the woods. And when Okonkwo goes to the cave to help his wife and protect their daughter, he displays behavior uncharacteristic of him—a man who uses village tradition to a fault in killing Ikemefuna.

The priestess Chielo continues to refer to Ezinma as "my daughter," suggesting a relationship that may lead Chielo to choose Ezinma as a priestess. She has twice before acknowledged that Ezinma may have special status because she was, but is no longer, an ogbanje (see Chapters 6 and 9).

Glossary

snuff   a preparation of powdered tobacco that is inhaled by sniffing, is chewed, or is rubbed on the gums.

saltpeter   potassium nitrate; used in the preparation of snuff (also in gunpowder and fireworks).

Agbala do-o-o-o! . . . Ezinmao-o-o-o   Chielo, the priestess, takes on the voice of the divine Agbala to ask for Ezinma to come to her.

Tufia-a!   This sound represents spitting and cursing simultaneously.

Chapter 12

Summary

After Chielo took Ezinma away, Okonkwo was not able to sleep. He made several trips to the cave before he finally found and joined Ekwefi waiting outside the cave. When Chielo came out of Agbala's cave with Ezinma in the early morning hours, she ignored Okonkwo and Ekwefi and carried the sleeping Ezinma home to her bed, with the girl's parents following behind.

On the following day, the village celebrates the next event in the marriage of the daughter of Obierika, Okonkwo's friend. The *uri* is a ritual in which the suitor presents palm-oil to everyone in the bride's immediate family, her relatives, and her extended group of kinsmen. For this ceremony, primarily a woman's ritual, the bride's mother is expected to prepare food for the whole village with the help of other women.

Ekwefi is exhausted after the preceding night's events. She delays going to the celebration until Ezinma wakes and eats her breakfast. Okonkwo's other wives and children proceed to Obierika's compound; the youngest wife promises to return to prepare Okonkwo's afternoon meal.

Obierika is slaughtering two goats for the soup and is admiring another goat that was bought in a neighboring village as a gift to the in-laws. He and the other men discuss the magic of medicine used in the other village that draws people to the market and helps rob some of them. While the women are preparing for the feast, they hear a cry in the distance, revealing that a cow is loose. Leaving a few women to tend the cooking, the rest go find the cow and drive it back to its owner, who must pay a heavy fine. The women check among themselves to be sure that every available woman has participated in rounding up the cow.

The palm-wine ceremony begins in the afternoon as soon as everyone gathers and begins to drink the first-delivered wine. When the new in-laws arrive, they present Obierika's family with fifty pots of wine, a very respectable number. The uri festivities continue into the night and end with much singing and dancing.

Commentary

Style & Language

This chapter further contributes to the understanding of several tribal customs and beliefs: the uri ceremony, which illustrates the phase of the marriage process following the agreement on bride-price (Chapter 8); the belief in supernatural powers to attract people to a market and even to help rob them; the law that requires villagers to control and corral their animals or else pay a penalty; and the custom that requires all available women to chase an escaped cow home. These descriptions follow the events of the preceding chapter and illustrate the strength of the villagers' beliefs in the earth goddess and her powers, even when she requires the near abduction of a child.

Yet, in most of the traditional events, the less than complete, blind obedience to a law or custom by some men and women suggests several strong, individual personalities. For example, Ekwefi is certainly one of the less-traditionally constrained women, and Obierika represents men who question some traditions and rituals.

Sexual activity is a subtle part of courtship and marriage rituals. The chant at the end of the celebration, "when I hold her waist beads / She pretends not to know," suggests that sexual anticipation is an enjoyable game for women as well as for men. In the preceding chapter, Okonkwo's protective, manly presence in the darkness by the cave triggers Ekwefi's fond memories of her first wedding night, when he "carried her into his bed and . . . began to feel around her waist for the loose end of her cloth."

Glossary

umunna   the extended family and kinsmen.

a great medicine   a supernatural power or magic that may take the shape of a person. In the Umuike market, the medicine assumes the shape of an old woman with a beckoning, magical fan.

yam pottage   a watery gruel made of yams.

Chapter 13

Summary

In the dead of night, the sound of a drum and a cannon announce the death of Ezeudu, an important man in the village. Okonkwo shivers when he remembers that Ezeudu had warned him against playing a part in the killing of Ikemefuna.

Everyone in the village gathers for the funeral ceremony of a warrior who had achieved three titles in his lifetime, a rare accomplishment. During the ceremony, men dance, fire off guns, and dash about in a frenzy of wailing for the loss of Ezeudu. Periodically, the egwugwu spirits appear from the underworld, including a one-handed spirit who dances and brings a message for the dead Ezeudu. Before the burial, the dancing, drumming, and gunshots become increasingly intense.

Suddenly an agonized cry and shouts of horror are followed by silence. Ezeudu's sixteen-year-old son is found dead in a pool of blood in the midst of the crowd. When Okonkwo fired his gun, it exploded and a piece of iron pierced the boy's heart. In the history of Umuofia, such an accident has never occurred.

Okonkwo's accidental killing of a clansman is a crime against the earth goddess, and he knows that he and his family must leave Umuofia for seven years. As his wives and children cry bitterly, they hurriedly pack their most valuable belongings into head loads to be carried as they prepare to flee before morning to Mbanta, the village of his mother. Friends move Okonkwo's yams to Obierika's compound for storage.

After the family's departure the next morning, a group of village men, carrying out the traditional justice prescribed by the earth goddess, invade Okonkwo's compound and destroy his barn, houses, and animals. Okonkwo's friend Obierika mourns his departure and wonders why Okonkwo should be punished so severely for an accident. Again, Obierika ponders the old traditions, remembering his own twin children who were abandoned in the forest because of tribal tradition.

Commentary

Theme

In the literary tradition of the tragic hero, Okonkwo's undoing continues with his accidental killing of Ezeudu's son. Early in the chapter, Achebe foreshadows the event with Okonkwo's memory of Ezeudu's warning about not killing Ikemefuna. The author builds dramatic tension by describing an increasingly frenzied scene of dancing, leaping, shouting, drumming, and the firing of guns, as well as the frightening appearance of the egwugwu. The action climaxes with an explosion of gunfire and then comes to a stop with the phrase "All was silent." Achebe emphasizes the gravity of Okonkwo's crime by saying that in Umuofia "nothing like this had ever happened."

As in Chapter 8, Obierika quietly questions clan traditions—this time, the tradition demanding that Okonkwo be banished for seven years because of an accidental killing. He also questions the tribal abandonment of twins, remembering his own innocent children left to die in the forest.

Literary Device

The chapter includes several intimations of impending doom for the clan and its traditions. Achebe ends the chapter dramatically with the proverb, "If one finger brought oil, it soiled the others," suggesting that Okonkwo's crime may lead to the ultimate downfall of Umuofia itself.

Glossary

Go-di-di-go-go-di-go. Di-go-go-di-go   the sound of drumbeats on the *ekwe*, or drums.

esoteric   intended for or understood by only a chosen few, as an inner group of disciples or initiates (said of ideas, literature, and so).

raffia   1) a palm tree of Madagascar, with large, pinnate leaves. 2) fiber from its leaves, used as string or woven into baskets, hats, and so on.

Mbanta   The name means small town and is where Okonkwo's mother comes from, his motherland, beyond the borders of Mbaino (Ikemefuna's original home).

Part Two
Chapter 14

Summary

Okonkwo arrives in Mbanta to begin his seven-year exile. His maternal uncle, Uchendu, now a village elder, welcomes him. Uchendu guesses what has happened, listens to Okonkwo's story, and arranges for the necessary rituals and offerings. He gives Okonkwo a plot of land on which to build a compound for his household, and Okonkwo receives additional pieces of land for farming. Uchendu's five sons each give him three hundred seed-yams to start his farm.

Okonkwo and his family must work hard to develop a new farm, and the work gives him no pleasure because he has lost the vigor and motivation of his younger days. He knows he is merely "marking time" while he is in Mbanta. He grieves over his interrupted plan to become one of the lords of his clan in Umuofia and blames his chi for his failure to achieve lasting greatness. Uchendu senses Okonkwo's depression and plans to speak to him later.

Uchendu's twenty-seven children gather from far and near for an *isa-ifi* ceremony. This final marriage ritual will determine if the intended bride of Uchendu's youngest son has been faithful to him during their courtship. The isa-ifi ceremony is described in detail.

The next day, in front of all of his children, Uchendu speaks to Okonkwo about his discouragement and despair. Through a series of questions no one is able to answer, Uchendu helps them all understand why a man should return to his motherland when he is bitter and depressed. He advises Okonkwo to comfort his family and prepare them for his eventual return to Umuofia, and, meanwhile, to accept the support of his kinsmen while he is here. If Okonkwo denies the support of his motherland, he may displease the dead. Uchendu points out that many people suffer more serious setbacks than a seven-year exile.

Commentary

Literary Device

In this chapter, Achebe presents a paradox about the manly and womanly aspects of Okonkwo's circumstances. Okonkwo begins his exile deeply discouraged and unmotivated. While striving for even greater manliness, he committed a female murder—that is, he accidentally killed a boy during the funeral ceremony. Making things worse (in his mind), he has been exiled to the woman's side of his family. He thus feels that this transition is an extraordinary challenge to his manliness. His uncle reminds him, though, in the presence of his own large family, that Okonkwo should use the nurturing (womanly) quality of his motherland, accept his situation (which is, in fact, far less devastating than it could be), and recover. Okonkwo needs to maintain a positive, responsible leadership (including male and female qualities) of his own family in preparation for their eventual return to Umuofia. The womanly aspect of his mother's village is not to be ignored while Okonkwo waits for the right to return to his own manly village.

In earlier chapters, Okonkwo acknowledged the vital role of chi in his life. In this chapter, he seems to realize that his chi "was not made for great things"—a reluctant admission that he may not achieve everything he wants because his fate is predetermined. His acceptance of this possible limitation, however, does not last.

With the description of the isa-ifi ceremony, this chapter completes the reader's view of the complex Igbo marriage rituals.

Glossary

twenty and ten years   Igbo counting may not have a unique number for thirty, which is thus counted as twenty and ten. Similarly, in French, seventy is counted as sixty-ten, and eighty is four twenties.

It is female ochu.   Crimes are divided into male and female types. Okonkwo's accidental killing of Ezeudu's son is considered manslaughter and therefore a female crime.

the nuts of the water of heaven   hailstones.

isa-ifi   the ceremony in which the bride is judged to have been faithful to her groom.

umuada   daughters who have married outside the clan.

Chapter 15

Summary

During Okonkwo's second year in exile, his good friend Obierika and two other young men pay him a visit in Mbanta. After his introduction to Uchendu, Obierika relays tragic news about the village of Abame.

One day a white man rode into the village on a bicycle, which the villagers called an "iron horse." At first, the people ran away from the man, but the ones who were less fearful walked up to him and touched his white skin. The elders of Abame consulted their Oracle, which told them that the white man would destroy their clan, and others were on their way, coming like locusts. Confronting the villagers, the white man seemed only to repeat a word like "Mbaino," perhaps the name of the village he was looking for. They killed the white man and tied his bicycle to their sacred tree.

Weeks later, three other white men and a group of natives—"ordinary men like us"—came to the village while most villagers were tending their farms. After the visitors saw the bicycle on the tree, they left. Many weeks later, the whole clan was gathered at the Abame market and then surrounded by a large group of men; they shot and killed almost everyone. The village is now deserted.

Okonkwo and Uchendu agree that the Abame villagers were foolish to kill a man about whom they knew nothing. They have heard stories about white men coming with guns and strong drink and taking slaves away across the sea, but they never believed the stories.

After their meal together, Obierika gives Okonkwo the money that he received for selling some of Okonkwo's yams and seedyams. He promises to continue giving Okonkwo the profits until he returns to Umuofia—or until "green men [come] to our clan and shoot us."

Commentary

Recall from Chapter 8 the joking reference to white men as lepers. Now, in Chapter 15, Obierika tells a story of how the first white man ever seen in Abame is initially a matter of curiosity, especially his skin color and perhaps his bicycle. When the villagers consult their Oracle, however, it predicts that white men will be instruments of disaster for the clan. Only then do the villagers take violent action against this individual white man, an action criticized as premature by Uchendu. Although Okonkwo agrees that the men of Abame were foolish for killing the white man, his response, "They should have armed themselves with their guns and their machetes even when they went to the market," illustrates that Okonkwo defies the Umuofian custom not to resort to violence without first trying to negotiate a peaceful settlement and seeking the acceptance of war by its Oracle. The Oracle never accepted a war with the white men, but it warned the villagers that the white men would spread destruction like "locusts." Ironically, the white men represent the coming of the locusts from Revelation in the Bible; the village will be destroyed, and among the villagers who aren't harmed, nothing good will come to them.

Of course, the retaliation by a large group of white men later—wiping out the entire village—is out of proportion to the initial crime. But this excessive action is Achebe's way of beginning the novel's characterization of extremist whites and their oppressive, often uninformed and insensitive attitude toward the natives. From this point on, the two groups are depicted as adversaries, and future conflict seems inevitable.

The Abame disaster is based on an actual event in 1905, in the community of Ahiara. More information about the incident and its consequences appears in the earlier section "A Brief History of Nigeria."

The chapter ends with a light-hearted exchange between Okonkwo and Obierika. When Obierika states, "Then kill yourself," this statement foreshadows Okonkwo's fatal ending.

Glossary

albino a person whose skin, hair, and eyes lack normal coloration because of genetic factors: albinos have a white skin, whitish hair, and pink eyes.

Eke day, Afo day The Igbo week has four days: Eke, Oye, Afo, and Nkwo.

iron horse the bicycle that the white man was riding when he apparently got lost.

Chapter 16

Summary

Two more years pass before Obierika visits Mbanta a second time, again with unhappy news. White Christian missionaries have arrived in Umuofia, have built a Christian church, and have recruited some converts. The leaders of the clan are disappointed in the villagers, but the leaders believe that the converts are only *efulefu*, the worthless and weak men of the village. None of the converts holds a title in the clan.

Obierika's real reason for the visit is to inform Okonkwo that he saw Nwoye with some missionaries in Umuofia. When Obierika asked Nwoye why he was in the village, Nwoye responded that he was "one of them." When asked about his father, Okonkwo, Nwoye replied that "he is not my father."

Okonkwo will not talk to his friend about Nwoye. Only after talking with Nwoye's mother is Obierika able to learn what happened: Six men arrived in Mbanta, including one white man. Everyone was curious to see him after hearing the story of the Abame destruction. The white man had an Igbo interpreter—with a strange dialect—and, through him, spoke to them about Christianity. He told them about a new god who created the world and humankind; this new god would replace the false gods of wood and stone that they had worshiped. Worship of the true god would ensure that they would live forever in the new god's kingdom. The white man told them that he and his people would be coming to live with them and would be bringing many iron horses for the villagers to ride.

The villagers asked many questions. When the missionary insisted that their gods were deceitful and arbitrary, the crowd began to move away. Suddenly, the missionaries began singing a joyful hymn and captured their attention once again.

Okonkwo decided that the man spoke nonsense and walked away. But Nwoye was impressed with the compassion of the new religion. It seemed to answer his questions about customs that included the killing of twins and Ikemefuna.

Commentary

Obierika is able to understand Nwoye's blunt statement only after he talks to Nwoye's mother. Her story may be sympathetically narrated because she is protective of Nwoye.

The Christian missionaries seem to win over many people of Mbanta rather quickly. The earliest converts are people with low status in the clan. The missionaries' promises fill a void in the lives of such converts. The Christian hymn, for example, touches the "silent and dusty chords in the heart of an Ibo man." (The old-style spelling of *Ibo* is used in the text; the modern spelling is *Igbo*.) Also note that the white man is not personalized yet—he remains a stereotype of a white missionary, though somewhat more patient in his responses than one may expect.

Considering the fate of the Abame village after the arrival of the white men, Mbanta's welcome of the missionaries isn't surprising. The presence of only one white person among the missionaries may have eased the villager's fears of the missionaries. The villagers are understandably skeptical about the Christian message but still curious to learn more about the strange religion and white skin with which they are unfamiliar. In addition, the missionaries' use of rhythmic, evangelistic hymns is a good seductive strategy for expanding their message through a sympathetic medium. They also promise new experiences, such as riding a bicycle, once they move into the community.

Unsurprisingly, Nwoye is highly receptive to the new, more humane-appearing doctrine, because he is a sensitive young man with deep concerns about certain customs of his people (see Chapter 7).

Achebe provides a humorous illustration of the difficulties of dialects, even within the Igbo language. The missionary's translator is an Igbo, but he speaks a dialect that pronounces some words and expressions differently from Umuofian Igbo: The word "myself" comes out as "my buttocks," resulting in some humorous translations of the white man's message.

Glossary

efulefu   worthless men in the eyes of the community.

evangelism   a preaching of, or zealous effort to spread, the gospel.

Jesu Kristi   Jesus Christ.

callow   young and inexperienced; immature.

Chapter 17

Summary

Chapter 17 continues the story of how Nwoye becomes a Christian. The missionaries sleep in the Mbanta marketplace for several nights and preach the Christian gospel each morning. After several days, they ask the leaders of the clan for land on which to build a church. The elders agree to give them a part of the Evil Forest, where people who died of evil diseases are buried, as well as the magical objects of great medicine men. The elders think that the missionaries are fools for taking the cursed land; according to tradition, the missionaries will be dead in a few days.

To the villagers' surprise and disappointment, the missionaries build their church without difficulty. The people of Mbanta begin to realize that the white man possesses incredible magic and power, especially because the missionaries and the church survived twenty-eight days—the longest period the gods allow a person to defy them. The missionaries soon acquire more converts, including their first woman—pregnant and previously the mother to four sets of twins, all of whom were abandoned in the forest. The white missionary moves on to Umuofia, while his interpreter, Mr. Kiaga, assumes responsibility for the Mbanta congregation.

As the number of converts grows, Nwoye secretly becomes more attracted to the religion and wants to attend Sunday church service, but he fears the wrath of his father if he enters the church.

One day, Okonkwo's cousin sees Nwoye inside the Christian church. He rushes to tell Okonkwo, who says nothing until his son returns home. In a rage, he asks Nwoye where he has been, but he gives no answer. When he starts to beat Nwoye with a heavy stick, his uncle Uchendu demands that Okonkwo leave his son alone. Nwoye leaves the hut and never returns. Instead, Nwoye moves to Umuofia, where the white missionary started a school for young people. He plans to return someday to convert his mother, brothers, and sisters.

At first, Okonkwo is furious with his son's action, but he concludes that Nwoye is not worth his anger. Okonkwo fears that, after his death, his younger sons will abandon the family ancestors because they have become attracted to the new religion. Okonkwo wonders how he gave life to such a foolish and womanly son, one who resembles his grandfather, Unoka, in so many ways.

Commentary

Theme

As the Christians begin to gain power, the villagers see their traditional beliefs as increasingly outdated and powerless. For example, Mbanta's Evil Forest proves to be less sinister than they have believed; their gods allow the missionaries to escape punishment. Here, Achebe implies that clinging to old traditions and an unwillingness to change may contribute to their downfall. Achebe does not pass judgment on their point of view, but he illustrates the kinds of circumstances that could make things fall apart.

The missionaries are beginning to influence not only the community's religious views and practices but also its deeper social customs and traditions; for example, they welcome the first female convert, a woman who is scorned by the community because of her four sets of twins. To her, as well as to other early converts shunned by the clan for one reason or another, the missionaries provide support and acceptance. The missionaries will not throw away newborn twins, and the community will eventually see that they are as normal as other children.

The missionaries apparently expect the new Christians in the community to accept a new weekly calendar: "Come [to church] every seventh day." Suddenly, the narrative refers to "Sunday" instead of the Igbo days of the week. Did the missionaries know about the Igbo four-day week? Did they preach the seven-day creation story? Consider the impact on a community when outsiders impose a new arrangement of days and weeks.

Character Insight

Okonkwo's violent reaction to Nwoye's conversion is typical; he immediately wants to kill the Christians. He recalls that he is popularly called the "Roaring Flame." Then he blames the "effeminacy" of his son on his wife and his father and then on his own chi. The last line in the chapter suggests that Okonkwo has an insight: "Living fire begets cold, impotent ash"—perhaps a realization that his own "Roaring Flame" behavior leaves behind coldness and powerlessness in others—as it has in his son.

Glossary

fetish   any object believed by some person or group to have magical power.

impudent   shamelessly bold or disrespectful; saucy; insolent.

Chapter 18

Summary

Initially, the church and the clan remain segregated from one another in Mbanta. The people of the village believe that eventually the Christians will weaken and die, especially since they live in the dreaded forest, where they even rescue twins abandoned in the woods.

One day, three converts come into the village saying that the traditional gods are dead, and the converts are ready to burn their shrines. The clan men severely beat the converts, after which nothing happens between the Christians and the clan for a long time. Eventually, rumors circulate that the church has set up its own government. But the villagers remain unconcerned about the church—until a new issue emerges.

The outcasts of Mbanta, the *osu*, live in a special section of the village and are forbidden to marry a free person or cut their hair. They are to be buried in the Evil Forest when they die. When the osu see that the church welcomes twins into their congregation, they think that they may be welcome also. After two outcasts attend service, other converts protest, saying that Mr. Kiaga does not understand the disgrace of associating with osu. But Mr. Kiaga says that the osu need the church more than anyone, and so he welcomes them, instructing them to shave off their mark of shame—their dirty, tangled hair. One prior convert chooses to return to the clan, but the others find strength and understanding in the missionaries' point of view. Most other osu become Christians, and the outcasts become the most dedicated members of the congregation.

A year later, one of the osu converts named Okoli is rumored to have killed the sacred python, the clan's most respected animal. The clan rulers and elders gather in Mbanta to decide on a punishment for the crime that they believed would never happen. Okonkwo, who has gained a leadership role in his motherland, believes the clan should react with violence, but the elders opt more peacefully to exclude church members from all aspects of clan life, much to Okonkwo's disgust.

The proclamation of exclusion keeps the Christians from the market, the stream, the chalk quarry, and the red earth pit. From the beginning,

Okoli denies killing the python, but then he cannot speak for himself because he is ill; by the end of the day, he dies. The villagers see his death as an act of revenge by the gods, so they agree not to bother the Christians.

Commentary

Okonkwo's views toward the Christians and his desire for a violent solution begin to separate him from the rest of his new Mbanta clan—which he thinks is a womanly clan. He feels that simply excluding the Christians from several public places is a weak solution.

Hoping not to come into conflict with one another, the church and the village are delicately maintaining an equilibrium by avoiding each other. When they do encounter each other, violence sometimes erupts, as when the three converts make fun of the old gods. In addition, as more new converts strengthen the church, they in turn weaken the clan, causing increased tension among the non-Christians as well as between the Christians and the non-Christians. When the church violates something sacred in the clan tradition, the precarious balance between church and clan is upset—a balance that is increasingly more difficult to maintain. Yet, even this crisis is resolved without violence.

The increasing strength of the new church is represented by the considerable preparations being made for the Christian Holy Week and Easter.

Glossary

osu   a class of people in Igbo culture considered outcasts, not fit to associate with free-born members of the clan.

caste   rigid class distinction based on birth, wealth, and so on, operating as a social system or principle.

heathen   anyone not a Jew, Christian, or Muslim; especially, a member of a tribe, nation, etc. worshiping many gods.

python   a very large, nonvenomous snake of Asia, Africa, and Australia, that squeezes its prey to death.

defecates   excretes waste matter from the bowels.

ostracize   to banish, bar, exclude, etc. from a group through rejection by general consent of the members.

Chapter 19

Summary

Although Okonkwo has achieved status in his motherland, he feels that his seven years in exile have been wasted. He could have risen to the peak of Umuofian society if he had not been forced into exile. At the beginning of his last year in Mbanta, Okonkwo sends money to Obierika in Umuofia to rebuild two huts on the site of his burned-out compound. He will build the remainder when he returns in a year.

As the time approaches for his family's return to Umuofia, Okonkwo instructs his wives and children to prepare a huge feast for his mother's kinsmen in Mbanta in a gesture to show his gratitude for kindness over the years of exile. Invited to the feast are all the living descendants of an ancestor who lived two hundred years earlier. Family members pick and prepare vegetables, slaughter goats and fowl, and prepare traditional dishes.

At the feast, Uchendu is honored as the oldest man at the feast; he breaks the kola nut and prays for health and children. As they drink wine, one of the oldest members of the clan thanks Okonkwo for his generosity in providing the magnificent feast. He then addresses the young people of the clan, disheartened at seeing the bonds of family and village breaking down as the Christians pull so many of the clan away, even from within families. He fears for the future of the young people and for the survival of the clan itself.

Commentary

Okonkwo's final days in Mbanta are characterized by his usual striving to impress, never doing anything by halves. He expresses his thanks to his motherland's relatives with an extravagant celebration. Okonkwo's rigid, impulsive behavior hasn't changed during his seven years in Mbanta, and he is eager to return to Umuofia to make up for lost time. He reveres Umuofia because of its strong and masculine community, unlike Mbanta, which he labels a womanly clan.

Achebe ends the chapter and Part Two with a foreshadowing of what is to follow: An elder member of the clan tells the young people, "I fear for you; I fear for the clan."

Glossary

wherewithal   that with which something can be done; necessary means.

egusi   melon seeds prepared for a soup.

I cannot live on the bank of a river and wash my hands with spittle. One must act according to one's fortune and circumstances; spittle is one's spit.

umunna   the extended family, the clan.

Part Three
Chapter 20

Summary

During Okonkwo's first year in exile, he already began to plan his grand return to Umuofia. Now he is determined to compensate for the seven years he considers wasted. Not only will he build a bigger compound than before, but he will also build huts for two new wives.

His plans for a triumphant return, however, are momentarily disrupted when Nwoye joins the Christians. At first, his oldest son's action depresses him. But he is confident that his other five sons will not disappoint him. Okonkwo also takes pride in his daughters, especially Ezinma, who has grown into a beautiful young woman. Her periods of illness are almost nonexistent. Many suitors in Mbanta have asked for her hand in marriage, but she has refused them all, knowing that her father wishes her to marry in Umuofia. Moreover, she has encouraged her half-sister Obiageli to do the same.

When Okonkwo returns to his village in Umuofia, he finds it greatly changed in his absence. The Christian church has won many converts, including respected men who have renounced their traditional titles. The white men have established a government court of law in Umuofia, where they try people who break the white men's laws; they have also built a prison, where lawbreakers are sent for punishment. The white men even employ natives as their "court messengers" to do the dirty work of arresting, guarding, and administering punishment to offending citizens.

Okonkwo wonders why his fellow Umuofians do not use violence to rid themselves of the white man's church and oppressive government. His friend Obierika says that they fear a fate like Abame's, the village destroyed by the white intruders. He also tells Okonkwo about a villager who was hanged by the government because of an argument over a piece of land. He points out that any violence will pit clansmen against one another, because many clan members have already joined the church. Obierika reflects on how the white men settled in quietly with their religion and then stayed to govern harshly, without ever learning the language or customs and without listening to reason.

Commentary

Okonkwo's concern about his status when he returns to Umuofia suggests that status and mobility within Umuofian society is largely self-determined: All males except outcasts have opportunities to move upward in the clan through hard work, wise use of resources, and gaining titles. Prominent status is essential to Okonkwo in his drive for manliness. Out of the community for seven years, Okonkwo lost his status among the village elders and the other egwugwu, and he has fallen behind in obtaining titles in the clan. He can compensate by making a show of his larger compound, more barns, and more wives and by starting to initiate his sons (besides Nwoye) into gaining titles—something few men can afford to do. He seems to be suppressing his sorrow over the loss of Nwoye and his disappointment about the loss of community position by reaffirming his beliefs in traditional Igbo ways and taking traditional steps toward recognition.

In light of his near obsession with status and titles, Okonkwo must find it particularly hard to understand how some of the leaders of the community can give up their titles when they became Christians.

Literary Device

In Part Two of the book, the major change introduced by the white man was the Christian church, which not only divided the community, but divided families. In the first chapter of Part Three, the white man's government assumes a central role, not only with its court and its "court messengers" but also with its prison and its executions. These changes are reported by Achebe in an ironic tone, as if the establishment of a government by the white colonialists was the Igbos' first experience with government, as if the Igbo did not have a justice system prior to the arrival of the whites. This tone is especially ironic because, earlier, Achebe takes great pains to illustrate not only the varieties of justice meted out by the Oracle (Okonkwo's banishment) and by the general citizenry (reprimands about violating the Week of Peace and about women not helping in the recovery of a stray cow), but he also illustrates the processes followed and the types of justice meted out by the formal court (Chapter 10). Remember that one of Achebe's goals in writing this novel was to demonstrate that the Igbo had developed a sophisticated society, religion, and justice system long before the Europeans arrived.

Achebe describes a colonial government that subdues the Igbo people without requiring the missionaries to learn their language or try to understand the Igbo traditions and ways. (The first church representative, Mr. Brown, is the exception in being accommodating to Igbo language and customs.)

By recruiting other African natives—the *kotmas*, or court messengers—to be their agents in the day-to-day enforcement of their authority, the missionaries bring into their use people with skin color and language characteristics much like the local natives—people who seem to be friends of the local natives (though their dialect was apparently different). Ultimately, the court messengers abused their positions by beating prisoners and taking bribes. Achebe is implying that corruption among the Igbo people isn't exclusive to Umuofia; the court messengers are more interested in what they can get out of the situation rather than what they can do to spread Christianity or even to help the Umuofians.

When Okonkwo tells Obierika that his fellow Umuofians should rise up against the British, Obierika wisely understands that it is too late. Many Umuofians have already "joined the ranks of the stranger." Obierika says that the white man "has put a knife on the things that held us together and we have fallen apart"—the first specific acknowledgment of the book's title, *Things Fall Apart*.

Glossary

anklet of his titles   When a man achieves a title, he wears a special anklet to indicate his title. He may wear more than one anklet to indicate more titles.

sacrament of Holy Communion   the most sacred ritual of participating Christians.

court messengers   the native Africans hired by the British to carry out their law enforcement activities; also called *kotma*. Kotma is a Pidgin English word derived from the words court and messenger.

Chapter 21

Summary

Not all members of the Igbo clan in Umuofia dislike the changes taking place. The Europeans are bringing wealth to the village as they begin to export palm-oil and palm nut kernels.

The white missionary, Mr. Brown, takes time to learn about the Igbo form of worship, often discussing religion with one of the elders of the clan. The two men debate the forms, actions, and attitudes of their respective gods. Mr. Brown restrains overeager members of his church from provoking villagers who cling to the old ways. Through his gentle patience, Mr. Brown becomes friends with some of the clan leaders, who begin to listen to and understand his message.

Mr. Brown urges the people of the clan to send their children to his school. He tells them that education is the key to maintaining control of their land. Eventually, people of all ages begin to listen to his message and attend his school. Mr. Brown's crusade gains power for the whites and for the church, but his diligence takes its toll on his health. He is forced to leave his congregation and return home.

Before Mr. Brown goes home, he visits Okonkwo to tell him that Nwoye—now called Isaac—has been sent to a teaching college in a distant town. Okonkwo drives the missionary out and orders him never to return.

Everything about the changed community of Umuofia displeases Okonkwo. His homecoming was not what he had hoped; no one really took much notice of his arrival. He can't even proceed with the ceremonies for his sons, because the rites are held only once every three years, and this year is not one of them. The dissolution of the old way of life saddens him as he sees the once fierce Umuofians becoming more and more "soft like women." He mourns for the clan, "which he saw breaking up and falling apart"—a phrase that again recalls the book's title.

Commentary

In this chapter, a third institution is established by the British in Umuofia—trade with the outside world. The Europeans buy palm-oil and palm kernels from the Igbo at a high price, and many Umuofians profit from the trade. These Umuofians welcome the new trading opportunities, though these activities are effectively undermining the clan and its self-sufficiency. Through narrative that gradually introduces these key, outside influences—religion, government, and commerce—Achebe shows how the British convinced so many Umuofians to welcome them in spite of their disruption of daily life and customs.

Indeed, the British seem to provide advantages lacking in Umuofian culture. The established members of the village welcome new opportunities for wealth. At the other end of the social scale, the disenfranchised members of Igbo society find acceptance in Christianity that they didn't experience in the so-called old ways. Mr. Brown builds a school and a much-needed small hospital in Umuofia; both institutions produce immediate and impressive results.

So the Umuofians now have more. Are they better off because of these additions to their lives? The British thought so and expected them to agree.

Achebe has said that he may have unconsciously modeled Mr. Brown, the white missionary, after G.T. Basden, a real-life missionary who worked among the Igbo in the early twentieth-century—a man who was a friend of Achebe's parents. Like Brown, Basden was a patient man who was willing to learn about so-called heathen traditions and values. However, Basden ultimately misunderstood Igbo culture, writing in *Among the Ibos of Nigeria* (1921) that "the black man himself does not know his own mind. He does the most extraordinary things, and cannot explain why he does them. . . . He is not controlled by logic."

Glossary

the new dispensation   the new system; the new organization of society under British influence.

kernels   the inner, softer part of a nut, fruit pit, etc. Here, found in the fleshy remains of the palm nut after its husk is crushed for palm-oil. The kernels can be processed by machine for the extraction of a very fine oil.

Ikenga   a carved wooden figure kept by every man in his shrine to symbolize the strength of a man's right hand.

Chukwu   the leading god in the Igbo hierarchy of gods.

the D.C.   the District Commissioner.

singlets   men's undershirts, especially the sleeveless kind.

Chapter 22

Summary

The new head of the Christian church, the Reverend James Smith, possesses nothing of Mr. Brown's compassion, kindness, or accommodation. He despises the way that Mr. Brown tried to lead the church. Mr. Smith finds many converts unfamiliar with important religious ideas and rituals, proving to himself that Mr. Brown cared only about recruiting converts rather than making them Christians. He vows to get the church back on the narrow path and soon demonstrates his intolerance of clan customs by suspending a young woman whose husband mutilated her dead ogbanje child in the traditional way. The missionary does not believe that such children go back into the mother's womb to be born again, and he condemns people who practice these beliefs as carrying out the work of the devil.

Each year, the Igbo clan holds a sacred ceremony to honor the earth deity. The *egwugwu*, ancestral spirits of the clan, dance in the tradition of the celebration. Enoch, an energetic and zealous convert, often provokes violent quarrels with people he sees as enemies. Approaching the egwugwu, who are keeping their distance from the Christians, Enoch dares the egwugwu to touch a Christian, so one of the egwugwu strikes him with a cane. Enoch responds by pulling the spirit's mask off, a serious offense to the clan because, according to Umuofian tradition, unmasking an egwugwu kills the ancestral spirit.

The next day, the egwugwu from all the villages gather in the marketplace. They storm Enoch's compound and destroy it with fire and machetes. Enoch takes refuge in the church compound, but the egwugwu follow him. Mr. Smith meets the men at the church door. Then the masked egwugwu begin to move toward the church, but they are quieted by their leader, who belittles Mr. Smith and his interpreter because they cannot understand what he is saying. He tells them that the egwugwu will not harm Mr. Smith for the sake of Mr. Brown, who was their friend. Mr. Smith will be able to stay safely in his house in Umuofia and worship his own god, but they intend to destroy the church that has caused the Igbo so many problems. Through his interpreter, Mr. Smith tries to calm them and asks that they leave the matter to him, but the egwugwu demolish his church to satisfy the clan spirit momentarily.

Commentary

Style & Language

Throughout the book Achebe gives his characters names with hidden meanings; for example, Okonkwo's name implies male pride and stubbornness. When Achebe adds British characters, he gives two of them common and unremarkable British names, Brown and Smith. His third British character, the District Commissioner, is known only by his title. The choice of names, and lack thereof, is in itself a commentary by Achebe on the incoming faceless strangers.

Achebe portrays Mr. Smith as a stereotype of the inflexible Christian missionary in Africa. He is a fire-and-brimstone type of preacher, who likens Igbo religion to the pagan prophets of Baal of the Old Testament and brands traditional Igbo beliefs as the work of the devil. Achebe suggests that the issue between Mr. Smith and the local people may be more than one of religion: "[Mr. Smith] saw things as black and white. And black was evil."

Mr. Smith preaches an uncompromising interpretation of the scriptures. He suspends a woman convert who allows an old Igbo belief about the ogbanje to contaminate her new Christian way of life. He labels this incident as "pouring new wine into old bottles," an act prohibited in the New Testament of the Christian Bible—"Neither do men put new wine into old bottles" (Matthew 9:17).

Achebe implies that strict adherence to scripture and dogma produces religious fanaticism. Enoch's unmasking of an egwugwu is portrayed as a result of unbridled fanaticism. In traditional Igbo religion, the ancestral spirit communicates through the mask in which it speaks. The Igbo believe that during this time, the human underneath the mask is not present; the mask is transformed into the spirit. Thus, unmasking the egwugwu kills the ancestral spirit. Enoch's action exposes the non-divine nature of an egwugwu, just a man beneath a mask, another sign of "things falling apart." Ironically, the outcome of Enoch's fanaticism must surely cause some clan members to question their long-held, sacred beliefs regarding the egwugwu.

Consistent with his high-energy radicalism, Enoch is disappointed that his action and its consequences do not provoke a holy war against the Igbo nonbelievers. "Holy war" was the term applied by zealot Christians of the twelfth and thirteenth centuries to the Crusades against the infidels, nonbelievers in Christianity.

Literary Device

The reference to the Mother of Spirits is another foreshadowing of the decline of the Umuofians. Her wailing and crying signals the death of "the very soul of the tribe." Enoch's unmasking of the egwugwu and the subsequent destruction of the church by the Igbo represent the climax of confrontation between traditional Igbo religious beliefs and British colonial Christianity, and, to a great extent, these events symbolize the broader cultural confrontation. Even the egwugwu leader acknowledges the cultural standoff between them: "We say he [Mr. Smith] is foolish because he does not know our ways, and perhaps he says we are foolish because we do not know his." Such an acknowledgment seems an indication that the Igbo are becoming resigned to their "new dispensation"—that they are moving toward a collective surrender to becoming civilized under the onslaught of forces far more organized and powerful than themselves.

Glossary

about sheep and goats / about wheat and tares   Two frequently quoted teachings of Jesus relate to the need for separating the good from the bad. In one, he refers to separating the sheep from the goats (Matthew 25:32); in the other, separating the wheat from the tares, or weeds (Matthew 13:30). Mr. Smith was obviously much concerned about dividing the community between the good (the Christian converts) and the bad (the traditional Igbo believers). Not coincidentally, his suspension of a convert is also based on a quotation from Matthew (9:17).

prophets of Baal   Mr. Smith is comparing the pagan worship of the warrior god Baal, mentioned in the Old Testament (I Kings 18) to the Igbo religion. The Israelites saw the worship of Baal as a rival to their worship of God, causing the prophet Elijah to challenge the prophets of Baal on Mount Carmel.

bull-roarer   a noisemaker made from a length of string or rawhide threaded through an object of wood, stone, pottery, or bone; a ritual device that makes a loud humming noise when swung rapidly overhead.

ogwu   medicine, magic.

desecrated   to have taken away the sacredness of; treat as not sacred; profane.

The body of the white man, I salute you.   The egwugwu speak indirectly, using a formal language of immortal spirits.

guttural   loosely, produced in the throat; harsh, rasping, and so on.

Chapter 23

Summary

Okonkwo is pleased about the destruction of the church and feels that daily life is beginning to seem normal again. For once, the clan listened to his advice and acted like warriors, though they didn't kill the missionary or drive the Christians out of Umuofia as he had urged.

When the District Commissioner returns from a trip and learns about the destruction of the church, he asks six leaders of the village, including Okonkwo, to meet with him in his government office. The six men agree but go to the meeting armed with their machetes.

The District Commissioner asks the village leaders, who have set their weapons aside, to explain their actions at the church to him and twelve other government men. As one of the leaders begins to tell about Enoch's unmasking of an egwugwu, the twelve government men surprise the clan leaders by handcuffing them and taking them into a guardroom.

The Commissioner reminds them that he and his government promote peace and want to help them be happy. When they treat others wrongly, they must be judged in the government court of law—the law of the Commissioner's "great queen." The leaders were wrong to hurt others and burn Enoch's house and the church. As a consequence, he says that they will be kept in prison, where they will be treated well and set free only after paying a fine of two hundred bags of cowries.

In prison, the guards repeatedly mistreat the six leaders, including shaving the men's heads. The prisoners sit in silence for two days without food, water, or toilet facilities. On the third day, in desperation, they finally talk among themselves about paying the fine. Okonkwo reminds them that they should have followed his advice and killed the white man when they had the chance. A guard hears him and hits them all with his stick.

As soon as the leaders were locked up, court messengers went around the village telling everyone that the prisoners would be released only after the village paid a fine of two hundred and fifty bags of cowries—

fifty of which the messengers would keep for themselves. Rumors circulated about possible hangings and shootings that occurred in Abame, including the families of the prisoners. At a town meeting, the Umuofians decide to collect the money immediately.

Commentary

This chapter describes the oppressive yet naive approach that the British took to ensure colonial justice. Although the District Commissioner says that he wants to hear both sides of the clan leaders' story, he doesn't trust the leaders and imprisons them while he collects a fine from the village. The Commissioner informs them that the British "have brought a peaceful administration to you and your people so that you may be happy." He may sincerely believe this statement, and he may also believe that the British control the court messengers when he assigns them as guards and as fine collectors. The court messengers (or *kotma*), however, not only abuse the prisoners, but they collect a fine considerably larger than what the Commissioner asks for so they can keep a sizable portion for themselves.

The District Commissioner's statements and personal actions are ironic in light of what is actually taking place: The British have decided that they know what is best for the Igbo and will go to violent and repressive lengths to bring their decision about. They justify their actions in the name of their great sovereign, Queen Victoria, "the most powerful ruler in the world."

Theme

A recurring theme underlying the occupation by the British is that the Africans are divided among themselves—an illustration of "divide and conquer." To help enforce their policies, the British employ other Africans to help them carry out their occupation and rule. The white colonialists apparently assume that their black subordinates would gain the confidence of the black natives. The British may not be aware that their court messengers, apparently Igbo, believe in customs, language, and values different from the Umuofians, and they already possess traditional antagonisms toward the Umuofian Igbo. Clearly, they do not understand Umuofian culture when they joke about so many Umuofians holding titles. They abuse their power by physically abusing their prisoners and asking the clan for an extra fifty bags of cowries for themselves. Because the court messengers are also the translators between the British and the Igbo, their opportunity for corruption is great. The

British who are aware of the brutality and corruption of their court messengers probably take refuge in the rationalization that the end—the ultimate civilizing of the natives—justifies the means.

The other method by which the British divide the Igbo is through the introduction of Christianity which, as one can see, results in the division of a community into opposing groups of citizens. Remember that the destruction of the church was triggered by the actions not of a white man, but of Enoch, a converted clansman—the ultimate irony.

Glossary

palaver   a conference or discussion, as originally between African natives and European explorers or traders.

a great queen   Queen Victoria, reigning head of the British Empire for sixty-four years (1837-1901).

Who is the chief among you?   The kotma (court messenger) guards see by the anklets that all six leaders own titles and joke that they must not be worth much.

Chapter 24

Summary

The District Commissioner sets the six men free after the village pays the required fine, and the leaders quietly return to their homes, deep in misery and not speaking to anyone they meet. Okonkwo's relatives and friends are waiting for him in his hut, and his friend Obierika urges him to eat the food his daughter Ezinma has prepared for him. No one else speaks, seeing the scars on his back where the prison guards beat him.

The same night, the village crier calls the clansmen to a meeting the next morning.

Okonkwo lies awake, thinking of his revenge. He hopes Umuofia will wage war on the intruders; if they don't, he will take action on his own. His anger turns on villagers who want to keep things peaceful instead of facing the need for war, even a "war of blame."

For the meeting in the marketplace, people come from even the farthest villages, except people who are friendly with the white foreigners. The first man to address the crowd is one of the leaders whom the Commissioner arrested. He calls for the village to take action against the unwanted strangers to rid themselves of the evil the strangers have brought. He admits that the Umuofians may have to fight and kill members of their own clan.

Suddenly, five court messengers approach the group. Okonkwo jumps forward to stop them. The messenger in charge says that the white man has ordered the meeting stopped. Okonkwo takes out his machete and beheads the man, but no one tries to stop the other messengers from escaping. The other clansmen are afraid, and someone asks, "Why did he do it?" Seeing such inaction and fear, Okonkwo cleans his machete on the sand and walks away, realizing that his fellow Umuofians will never go to war.

Commentary

After Okonkwo is freed from prison, he remembers better times, when Umuofia was more warrior-like and fierce—"when men were men." As in his younger days, he is eager to prepare for war (not unlike Enoch the convert in the preceding chapter). He is worried that the peacemakers among them may have a voice, but he assures himself that he will continue the resistance, even if he has to do it alone. He will be manly in his actions even to the end.

Umuofian culture has traditionally discriminated against women and other outcasts—and currently against Christian converts. This discrimination has marginalized many people, including even important "sons" of Umuofia. The speaker points out that not "all the sons of Umuofia" are with them at the vital clan gathering; he admits that they may have to kill their own clansmen if they go to war. Yet the speaker feels that they must do battle in order to rid themselves of this evil.

When Okonkwo kills the court messenger, his fellow clansmen almost back away from him in fear; in fact, his violent action is questioned. When he realizes that no one supports him, Okonkwo finally knows that he can't save his village and its traditions no matter how fiercely he tries. His beloved and honored Umuofia is on the verge of surrender, and Okonkwo himself feels utterly defeated. Everything has fallen apart for him. His action in the final chapter will not be a surprise.

Glossary

a war of blame In Chapter 2, the villagers state that a "fight of blame" (which Okonkwo expects the peacemakers to label this fight against the strangers) would never be sanctioned by their Oracle, which approves only a "just war." Therefore, what Okonkwo is considering may go beyond even the clan's traditions—a fight for which they may not have full justification from their gods.

creepers plants whose stems put out tendrils or rootlets by which they can creep along a surface as they grow.

Chapter 25

Summary

Following the killing of the messenger, the District Commissioner goes to Okonkwo's compound and, finding a small crowd, demands to see Okonkwo. Obierika repeatedly says that he is not home. When the Commissioner threatens the men, Obierika agrees to show him where Okonkwo is, expressing the hope that the Commissioner's men will help them.

Obierika leads the Commissioner and his men to an area behind the compound, where Okonkwo's body hangs lifeless from a tree—a victim of suicide. Obierika asks the Commissioner if his men will cut Okonkwo down from the tree and bury him. According to tradition, the people of the clan cannot touch the body of a man who killed himself—a sin against the earth. Obierika angrily accuses the Commissioner causing the death of his good friend. The Commissioner orders his men to take down the body and bring it and the crowd to the court.

As the Commissioner leaves, he thinks about the book in which he writes about his experiences in civilizing the people of Nigeria. He will possibly write a chapter, or perhaps an interesting paragraph, about the man who killed a messenger and then killed himself. The Commissioner will title his book *The Pacification of the Primitive Tribes of the Lower Niger*.

Commentary

Style & Language

The book's final confrontation between the District Commissioner and the Umuofians is almost anticlimactic. It serves to demonstrate once more the deep cultural gulf between the Europeans and the Igbos. This difference is dramatized not solely by the events but also by the language of the chapter. For example, notice the sudden appearance of several literate words relating to the Commissioner throughout the scene: infuriating, superfluous, instantaneously, resolute. He imagines himself to be a "student of primitive customs," listening to the explanation of the "primitive belief" about handling the body of a suicide.

His warning about the natives playing "monkey tricks" may reflect his views that they are, in fact, animalistic—perhaps like primates in the wild.

In preparation for the final paragraph of the novel, Achebe dramatically shifts the narrative style from an omniscient, mostly objective point of view to the personal point of view of the District Commissioner, whose thoughts in the final paragraph become the final irony of the book. The Commissioner sees himself as a benevolent ambassador to the natives—one who must maintain his dignity at all times in order to earn the favorable opinion of the natives. He prides himself on having spent many years toiling to bring "civilization to different parts of Africa," and he has "learned a number of things." The Commissioner feels that his experiences allow him the privilege of writing the definitive book on *The Pacification of the Primitive Tribes of the Lower Niger.*

Primitive is, of course, his British point of view. The Commissioner, like other colonialists, cannot imagine that he understands very little about the Igbo, especially that they are not primitive—except perhaps from a European technological perspective. In the meantime, the novel has revealed to its readers the complex system of justice, government, society, economy, religion, and even medicine in Umuofia before the British arrived.

Finally, the Commissioner seems unconcerned about the ironic fact that the colonialists' methods of pacification are often achieved through suppression and violence—themselves essentially primitive means for achieving nationalistic objectives.

Glossary

superfluous   being more than is needed, useful, or wanted; surplus; excessive.

monkey tricks   possibly a racial slur directed at the natives.

resolute   having or showing a fixed, firm purpose; determined; resolved; unwavering.

abomination   anything hateful and disgusting.

Yes, sah   *Yes sir;* the form may be Pidgin English and illustrates how the native-born court messengers submitted to the orders of their white bosses—at least on the surface.

CHARACTER ANALYSES

The following character analyses delve into the physical, emotional, and psychological traits of the literary work's major characters so that you might better understand what motivates these characters. The writer of this study guide provides this scholarship as an educational tool by which you may compare your own interpretations of the characters. Before reading the character analyses that follow, consider first writing your own short essays on the characters as an exercise by which you can test your understanding of the original literary work. Then, compare your essays to those that follow, noting discrepancies between the two. If your essays appear lacking, that might indicate that you need to re-read the original literary work or re-familiarize yourself with the major characters.

Okonkwo

The protagonist of *Things Fall Apart*, Okonkwo is also considered a tragic hero. A tragic hero holds a position of power and prestige, chooses his course of action, possesses a tragic flaw, and gains awareness of circumstances that lead to his fall. Okonkwo's tragic flaw is his fear of weakness and failure.

In his thirties, Okonkwo is a leader of the Igbo community of Umuofia. Achebe describes him as "tall and huge" with "bushy eyebrows and [a] wide nose [that gives] him a very severe look." When Okonkwo walks, his heels barely touch the ground, like he walks on springs, "as if he [is] going to pounce on somebody." Okonkwo "stammers slightly" and his breathing is heavy.

Okonkwo is renowned as a wrestler, a fierce warrior, and a successful farmer of yams (a "manly" crop). He has three wives and many children who live in huts on his compound. Throughout his life, he wages a never ending battle for status; his life is dominated by the fear of weakness and failure. He is quick to anger, especially when dealing with men who are weak, lazy debtors like his father. However, Okonkwo overcompensates for his father's womanly (weak) ways, of which he is ashamed, because he does not tolerate idleness or gentleness. Even though he feels inward affection at times, he never portrays affection toward anyone. Instead, he isolates himself by exhibiting anger through violent, stubborn, irrational behavior. Okonkwo demands that his family work long hours despite their age or limited physical stamina, and he nags and beats his wives and son, Nwoye, who Okonkwo believes is womanly like his father, Unoka.

Okonkwo is impulsive; he acts before he thinks. Consequently, Okonkwo offends the Igbo people and their traditions as well as the gods of his clan. Okonkwo is advised not to participate in the murder of Ikefemuna, but he actually kills Ikefemuna because he is "afraid of being thought weak." When the white man brings Christianity to Umuofia, Okonkwo is opposed to the new ways. He feels that the changes are destroying the Igbo culture, changes that require compromise and accommodation—two qualities that Okonkwo finds intolerable. Too proud and inflexible, he clings to traditional beliefs and mourns the loss of the past.

When Okonkwa rashly kills a messenger from the British district office, his clansmen back away in fear; he realizes that none of them support him and that he can't save his village from the British colonists. Okonkwo is defeated. He commits suicide, a shameful and disgraceful death like his father's.

Unoka

A tall, thin man with a slight stoop, Unoka was Okonkwo's father. He appeared "haggard and mournful . . . except when he was drinking or playing his flute." His favorite time of year was after the harvest when he joined with village musicians to make music and feast; Unoka's priority was to enjoy life to the fullest. An excellent flutist, he was happy and peaceful when he was playing his flute, in spite of the sorrow and grief that was evident in his music.

Unoka lacked responsibility. He was poor, lazy, and neglectful of his wife, and he did not plan for the future. During his life, he never took a title and, therefore, never gained status or respect from the villagers. Instead, they called him a loafer, and he was the laughingstock of the community. Whenever he managed to get his hands on money, "he immediately bought gourds of palm-wine." Unoka was a debtor and a failure. Also a coward, he never became a warrior—wars made him unhappy because he couldn't stand the sight of blood. Unoka's behavior was contrary to typical Igbo tradition, so he was not taken seriously and was treated in a demeaning manner by Igbo clansmen and, later, by Okonkwo, his son.

Evil fortune seemed to follow Unoka to his grave. He died of a horrible illness—a swelling of the stomach and limbs—and was left to die above ground in the Evil Forest.

Obierika

Okonkwo's best friend, Obierika serves as a foil for Okonkwo. That is, Obierika's personality contrasts with and enhances the distinctive characteristics of Okonkwo's personality. Obierika is a reasonable person who thinks before he acts, unlike Okonkwo, who is impulsive. Obierika does not advocate the use of violence to get revenge against the British colonizers—Okonkwo does. Obierika is open-minded; he understands and appreciates the changing values and foreign culture that is infiltrating the Igbo traditions. Obierika is receptive to new ideas and is willing to adapt to change, whereas Okonkwo is narrow-minded, unable to accept any change to traditional Igbo culture and beliefs.

Even though the personalities of Obierika and Okonkwo are vastly different, Obierika supports Okonkwo as a friend. He comforts Okonkwo when Okonkwo is depressed over Ikemefuna's death, despite the fact that he disapproves of Okonkwo's role in Ikemefuna's murder. When Okonkwo goes into exile, Obierika sells Okonkwo's yams and seed-yams and gives Okonkwo the profits.

Unlike Okonkwo, Obierika questions the Igbo traditions and ritual, as well as their tribal law. He thinks that change may improve the Igbo society. Whereas Okonkwo's solution is to use violence against the British, Obierika understands that rising up against the British is too late. He comments that the white man "has put a knife on the things that have held us together and we have fallen apart."

Mr. Brown

Mr. Brown is the first white Christian missionary in Umuofia and Mbanta. He is a patient, kind, and understanding man. He is also open-minded and willing to make an effort to respect and understand the Igbo beliefs. Mr. Brown restrains overeager members of his church from provoking clan members; evidence that supports his shared belief with the Igbo people in the value of peaceful relations. He befriends many great men of the clan who begin to listen to and understand his message. He also discusses religious beliefs with Akunna, a clan leader of Umuofia. Neither man gives up his belief, but they learn about each other's faith and gain respect for one another.

Mr. Brown builds a school and a hospital in Umuofia. He urges the Igbo people to send their children to school and makes a point of giving gifts, such as singlets and towels to the children (and later to adults) who attend school. Mr. Brown tells the Igbo people that their future leaders will have to know how to read and write. He knows the British way—to do away with the traditional government of the Igbo people and instate their own form of government. Mr. Brown informs the Igbo people that they will need to adapt so they will not lose all their autonomy—and their traditional beliefs.

Reverend James Smith

Reverend Smith is a missionary who replaces Mr. Brown as the new head of the Christian church. Reverend Smith is strict and uncompromising, the opposite of Mr. Brown who was kind, compassionate, and accommodating.

Reverend Smith is a stereotypical fire-and-brimstone preacher: "He [sees] things as black and white. And black [is] evil." He is intolerant and disrespectful of Igbo beliefs and customs and likens Igbo religion to the pagan prophets of Baal of the Old Testament; he considers their beliefs to be the work of the devil. Reverend Smith demands that Igbo clansmen who convert to Christianity reject all indigenous beliefs. He is determined to follow a strict interpretation of the scriptures. Mr. Smith demonstrates his intolerance of Igbo beliefs when he suspends a woman convert from the Christian church who followed traditional custom regarding her dead ogbanje child.

Because Reverend Smith expects converts to adhere to all Christian scripture and dogma in a very narrow-minded manner, he incites converts to become overzealous, even fanatical, about their newfound belief. After Enoch, a zealous convert, creates a conflict during an Igbo ceremony, the *egwugwu*, or ancestral spirits of the clan, burn Enoch's compound and then proceed to the church compound. Reverend Smith, who has no idea why the egwugwu are upset (nor does he care), is unharmed only because of Mr. Brown's preceding compassion toward the Igbo people and his understanding of their beliefs. The egwugwu destroy Reverend Smith's church.

CRITICAL
ESSAYS

On the pages that follow, the writer of this study guide provides critical scholarship on various aspects of Achebe's *Things Fall Apart*. These interpretive essays are intended solely to enhance your understanding of the original literary work; they are supplemental materials and are not to replace your reading of *Things Fall Apart*. When you're finished reading *Things Fall Apart*, and prior to your reading this study guide's critical essays, consider making a bulleted list of what you think are the most important themes and symbols. Write a short paragraph under each bullet explaining why you think that theme or symbol is important; include at least one short quote from the original literary work that supports your contention. Then, test your list and reasons against those found in the following essays. Do you include themes and symbols that the study guide author doesn't? If so, this self test might indicate that you are well on your way to understanding original literary work. But if not, perhaps you will need to re-read *Things Fall Apart*.

Major Themes in the Novel

For many writers, the theme of a novel is the driving force of the book during its creation. Even if the author doesn't consciously identify an intended theme, the creative process is directed by at least one controlling idea—a concept or principle or belief or purpose significant to the author. The theme—often several themes—guides the author by controlling where the story goes, what the characters do, what mood is portrayed, what style evolves, and what emotional effects the story will create in the reader.

Igbo Society Complexity

From Achebe's own statements, we know that one of his themes is the complexity of Igbo society before the arrival of the Europeans. To support this theme, he includes detailed descriptions of the justice codes and the trial process, the social and family rituals, the marriage customs, food production and preparation processes, the process of shared leadership for the community, religious beliefs and practices, and the opportunities for virtually every man to climb the clan's ladder of success through his own efforts. The book may have been written more simply as a study of Okonkwo's deterioration in character in an increasingly unsympathetic and incompatible environment, but consider what would have been lost had Achebe not emphasized the theme of the complex and dynamic qualities of the Igbo in Umuofia.

Clash of Cultures

Against Achebe's theme of Igbo cultural complexity is his theme of the clash of cultures. This collision of cultures occurs at the individual and societal levels, and the cultural misunderstanding cuts both ways: Just as the uncompromising Reverend Smith views Africans as "heathens," the Igbo initially criticize the Christians and the missionaries as "foolish." For Achebe, the Africans' misperceptions of themselves and of Europeans need realignment as much as do the misperceptions of Africans by the West. Writing as an African who had been "Europeanized," Achebe wrote *Things Fall Apart* as "an act of atonement with [his] past, the ritual return and homage of a prodigal son." By his own act, he encourages other Africans, especially ones with Western educations, to realize that they may misperceive their native culture.

Destiny

Related to the theme of cultural clash is the issue of how much the flexibility or the rigidity of the characters (and by implication, of the British and Igbo) contribute to their destiny. Because of Okonkwo's inflexible nature, he seems destined for self-destruction, even before the arrival of the European colonizers. The arrival of a new culture only hastens Okonkwo's tragic fate.

Two other characters contrast with Okonkwo in this regard: Mr. Brown, the first missionary, and Obierika, Okonkwo's good friend. Whereas Okonkwo is an unyielding man of action, the other two are more open and adaptable men of thought. Mr. Brown wins converts by first respecting the traditions and beliefs of the Igbo and subsequently allowing some accommodation in the conversion process. Like Brown, Obierika is also a reasonable and thinking person. He does not advocate the use of force to counter the colonizers and the opposition. Rather, he has an open mind about changing values and foreign culture: "Who knows what may happen tomorrow?" he comments about the arrival of foreigners. Obierika's receptive and adaptable nature may be more representative of the spirit of Umuofia than Okonkwo's unquestioning rigidity.

For example, consider Umuofia's initial lack of resistance to the establishment of a new religion in its midst. With all its deep roots in tribal heritage, the community hardly takes a stand against the intruders—against new laws as well as new religion. What accounts for this lack of community opposition? Was Igbo society more receptive and adaptable than it appeared to be? The lack of strong initial resistance may also come from the fact that the Igbo society does not foster strong central leadership. This quality encourages individual initiative toward recognition and achievement but also limits timely decision-making and the authority-backed actions needed on short notice to maintain its integrity and welfare. Whatever the reason—perhaps a combination of these reasons—the British culture and its code of behavior, ambitious for its goals of native "enlightenment" as well as of British self-enrichment, begin to encroach upon the existing Igbo culture and its corresponding code of behavior.

A factor that hastens the decline of the traditional Igbo society is their custom of marginalizing some of their people—allowing the existence of an outcast group and keeping women subservient in their household and community involvement, treating them as property, and accepting physical abuse of them somewhat lightly. When representatives of a foreign culture (beginning with Christian missionaries) enter Igbo territory and accept these marginalized people—including the twins—at their full human value, the Igbo's traditional shared leadership finds itself unable to control its whole population. The lack of a clear, sustaining center of authority in Igbo society may be the quality that decided Achebe to draw his title from the Yeats poem, "The Second Coming." The key phrase of the poems reads, "Things fall apart; the center cannot hold."

Underlying the aforementioned cultural themes is a theme of *fate*, or destiny. This theme is also played at the individual and societal levels. In the story, readers are frequently reminded about this theme in references to *chi*, the individual's personal god as well as his ultimate capability and destiny. Okonkwo, at his best, feels that his *chi* supports his ambition: "When a man says yes, his chi says yes also" (Chapter 4). At his worst, Okonkwo feels that his chi has let him down: His chi "was not made for great things. A man could not rise beyond the destiny of his chi. . . . Here was a man whose chi said nay despite his own affirmation" (Chapter 14).

At the societal level, the Igbos' lack of a unifying self-image and centralized leadership as well as their weakness in the treatment of some of their own people—both previously discussed—suggest the inevitable fate of becoming victim to colonization by a power eager to exploit its resources.

In addition to the three themes discussed in this essay, the thoughtful reader will probably be able to identify other themes in the novel: for example, the universality of human motives and emotions across cultures and time, and the need for balance between individual needs and community needs.

Use of Language

Writers in Third World countries that were formerly colonies of European nations debate among themselves about their duty to write in their native language rather than in the language of their former colonizer. Some of these writers argue that writing in their native language is imperative because cultural subtleties and meanings are lost in translation. For these writers, a "foreign" language can never fully describe their culture.

Choosing a Language

Achebe maintains the opposite view. In a 1966 essay reprinted in his book *Morning Yet on Creation Day*, he says that, by using English, he presents "a new voice coming out of Africa, speaking of African experience in a world-wide language." He recommends that the African writer use English "in a way that brings out his message best without altering the language to the extent that its value as a medium of international exchange will be lost. [The writer] should aim at fashioning out an English which is at once universal and able to carry his peculiar experience." Achebe accomplishes this goal by innovatively introducing Igbo language, proverbs, metaphors, speech rhythms, and ideas into a novel written in English.

Achebe agrees, however, with many of his fellow African writers on one point: The African writer must write for a social purpose. In contrast to Western writers and artists who create art for art's sake, many African writers create works with one mission in mind—to reestablish their own national culture in the postcolonial era. In a 1964 statement, also published in *Morning Yet on Creation Day*, Achebe comments that: "African people did not hear of culture for the first time from Europeans. . . . their societies were not mindless, but frequently had a philosophy of great depth and value and beauty, . . . they had poetry, and above all, they had dignity. It is this dignity that African people all but lost during the colonial period, and it is this that they must now regain."

To further his aim of disseminating African works to a non-African audience, Achebe became the founding editor for a series on African literature—the African Writers Series—for the publishing firm Heinemann.

The Use of English

Achebe presents the complexities and depths of an African culture to readers of other cultures as well as to readers of his own culture. By using English—in which he has been proficient since childhood—he reaches many more readers and has a much greater literary impact than he would by writing in a language such as Igbo. Writers who write in their native language must eventually allow their works to be translated, often into English, so readers outside the culture can learn about it.

Yet by using English, Achebe faces a problem. How can he present the African heritage and culture in a language that can never describe it adequately? Indeed, one of the primary tasks of *Things Fall Apart* is to confront this lack of understanding between the Igbo culture and the colonialist culture. In the novel, the Igbo ask how the white man can call Igbo customs bad when he does not even speak the Igbo language. An understanding of Igbo culture can only be possible when the outsider can relate to the Igbo language and terminology.

Achebe solves this problem by incorporating elements of the Igbo language into his novel. By incorporating Igbo words, rhythms, language, and concepts into an English text about his culture, Achebe goes a long way to bridge a cultural divide.

The Igbo vocabulary is merged into the text almost seamlessly so the reader understands the meaning of most Igbo words by their context. Can any attentive reader of *Things Fall Apart* remain unfamiliar with words and concepts represented by *chi, egwugwu, ogbanje,* and *obi*? Such Igbo terms as chi and ogbanje are essentially untranslatable, but by using them in the context of his story, Achebe helps the non-Igbo reader identify with and relate to this complex Igbo culture.

Chi, for example, represents a significant, complex Igbo concept that Achebe repeatedly refers to by illustrating the concept in various contexts throughout the story. Achebe translates chi as *personal god* when he first mentions Unoka's bad fortune. As the book progresses, it gradually picks up other nuances. As discussed in the Commentary section for Chapter 3, the chi concept is more complex than a personal deity or even *fate*, another frequently used synonym. Chi suggests elements of the Hindu concept of karma, the concept of the soul in some Christian denominations, and the concept of individuality in some mystical philosophies. The understanding of chi and its significance in Igbo culture grows as one progresses through the book.

Another example of Achebe's incorporation of Igbo elements is his frequent reference to traditional Igbo proverbs and tales. These particular elements give *Things Fall Apart* an authentic African voice. The Igbo culture is fundamentally an oral one—that is, "Among the Igbo, the art of conversation is regarded very highly, and proverbs are the palm-oil with which words are eaten" (Chapter1). To provide an authentic feel for Igbo culture would be impossible without also allowing the proverbs to play a significant role in the novel. And despite the foreign origin of these proverbs and tales, the Western reader can relate very well to many of them. They are woven smoothly into their context and require only occasional explanation or elaboration. These proverbs and tales are, in fact, quite similar in spirit to Western sayings and fables.

Modern-day readers of this novel not only relate easily to traditional proverbs and tales but also sympathize with the problems of Okonkwo, Nwoye, and other characters. Achebe has skillfully developed his characters, and even though they live in a different era and a very different culture, one can readily understand their motivations and their feelings because they are universal and timeless.

Speech patterns and rhythms are occasionally used to represent moments of high emotion and tension. Consider the sound of the drums in the night in Chapter 13 (*go-di-di-go-go-di-go*); the call repeated several times to unite a gathering followed by its group response, first described in Chapter 2 (*Umuofia kwenu . . . Yaa!*); the agonized call of the priestess seeking Ezinma in Chapter 11 (*Agbala do-o-o-o!*); the repetitious pattern of questions and answers in the *isa-ifi* marriage ritual in Chapter 14; the long narrated tale of Tortoise in Chapter 11; and the excerpts from songs in several chapters.

Achebe adds another twist in his creative use of language by incorporating a few examples of Pidgin English. Pidgin is a simplified form of language used for communicating between groups of people who normally speak different languages. Achebe uses only a few Pidgin words or phrases—*tie-tie* (to tie); *kotma* (a crude form of court messenger); and *Yes, sah*—just enough to suggest that a form of Pidgin English was being established. As colonialists, the British were adept at installing Pidgin English in their new colonies. Unfortunately, Pidgin sometimes takes on characteristics of master-servant communication; it can sound patronizing on the one hand, and subservient on the other. Furthermore, using the simplified language can become an easy excuse for not learning the standard languages for which it substitutes.

Achebe's use of Igbo language, speech patterns, proverbs, and richly drawn characters creates an authentic African story that effectively bridges the cultural and historical gap between the reader and the Igbo. *Things Fall Apart* is a groundbreaking work for many reasons, but particularly because Achebe's controlled use of the Igbo language in an English novel extends the boundaries of what is considered English fiction. Achebe's introduction of new forms and language into a traditional (Western) narrative structure to communicate unique African experiences forever changed the definition of world literature.

Pronunciation of Igbo Names and Words

Like Chinese, the Igbo language is a tonal one; that is, differences in the actual voice pitch and the rise or fall of a word or phrase can produce different meanings. In Chapter 16, for example, Achebe describes how the missionary's translator, though an Igbo, can not pronounce the Mbanto Igbo dialect: "Instead of saying 'myself' he always said 'my buttocks.'" (The form <ac;a;I>k<ac;a;e> means *strength* while <ac;a;I>k<ac;g;e> means *buttocks*.)

Igbo names usually represent meanings—often entire ideas. Some names reflect the qualities that a parent wishes to bestow on a child; for example, Ikemefuna means *my power should not be dispersed*. Other names reflect the time, area, or other circumstances to which a child is born; for example, Okoye means *man born on Oye Day*, the second day of the Igbo week. And Igbo parents also give names to honor someone or something else; for instance, Nneka means *mother is supreme*.

Prior to Nigerian independence in 1960, the spelling of Igbo words was not standardized. Thus the word Igbo is written as *Ibo*, the pre-1960 spelling throughout *Things Fall Apart*. The new spellings reflect a more accurate understanding and pronunciation of Igbo words. The List of Characters includes a pronunciation that uses equivalent English syllables for most of the main characters' names.

CliffsNotes Review

Use this CliffsNotes Review to test your understanding of the original text and reinforce what you've learned in this book. After you work through the question and answer section, the identify the quote section, and the essay questions, you're well on your way to understanding a comprehensive and meaningful interpretation of *Things Fall Apart*.

Q&A

1. Okonkwo got help for planting yams when he began share cropping for _____.

2. Okonkwo distinguished himself and brought honor to his village when he wrestled _____.

3. Okonkwo and his family are exiled for _____ years.

4. The personal god that each individual is given by the creator at the moment of conception is _____.

5. Mr. Brown discusses religion with _____.

6. The spirits of the ancestors are known as _____.

7. The Christian missionary builds a church on land located in the _____.

8. Chielo takes Ezinma to see _____.

9. Okonkwo is welcomed in Mbanta by _____.

10. Okonkwo accidentally killed the son of _____.

Answers: (1) Nwakibie (2) Amalinze the Cat (3) seven (4) chi (5) Akunna (6) egwugwu (7) Evil Forest (8) Agbala (9) Uchendu (10) Ezeudu

Identify the Quote: Find Each Quote in *Things Fall Apart*

Identify the speaker and state the importance of the quote in the context of the entire work.

1. "If a child washed his hands he could eat with kings."

2. "When the moon is shining the cripple become hungry for a walk."

3. "A man who pays respect to the great paves the way for his own greatness."

4. "A toad does not run in the daytime for nothing."

5. "A chick that will grow into a cock can be spotted the very day it hatches."

Answers: (1) Narrator speaking about Okonkwo. If you work hard, you will be rewarded. (2) Narrator. The moonlight is irresistible. (3) Okonkwo speaking to Nwakibie. If Okonkwo wants greatness for himself, he must cater to people with greatness. (4) Ogbuefi Idigo talking about Obiako. Obiako must have had good reason to give up his trade. (5) Okonkwo speaking to Obierika. A boy that will become a man can be identified at birth.

Essay Questions

1. Why did Achebe choose to take the title of his novel, *Things Fall Apart*, from William Butler Yeats' poem "The Second Coming"?

2. What is the narrator's point of view and what values are important to the narrator?

3. Achebe presents details of daily village life in Umuofia, as well as details concerning the Igbo culture. Describe the setting of the novel.

4. What is *chi*? Explain the importance of chi in shaping Okonkwo's destiny.

5. Obierika is a foil for Okonkwo. That is, when compared to Okonkwo, the contrast between the two characters emphasizes the distinctive characteristics of Okonkwo. Compare the two characters—Obierika and Okonkwo.

6. Achebe suggests that Igbo culture is *dynamic* (constantly changing). Find evidence in the novel to support this notion.

7. What is the significance of Nwoye's Christian name, Isaac?

8. In *Things Fall Apart*, Achebe includes stories from Igbo culture and tradition, proverbs, and parables. What is the significance of Achebe's integration of African literary forms with that of Western literary forms?

9. Achebe resents the stereotype of African cultures that is presented in literature, such as *Heart of Darkness* by Joseph Conrad. Identify instances in *Things Fall Apart* that portray variations in African cultures.

10. What is the role of women in the novel?

11. Explain the advantages and disadvantages of the social structure portrayed in *Things Fall Apart*. For example, the culture is *polygamous*; the husband, wives, and children live in their own compound; children are cared for communally.

12. Explain why you think Okonkwo kills himself.

13. In your opinion, what contributes most to things falling apart in Umuofia? Explain.

14. How are the womanly or feminine qualities of the Igbo culture important to its survival?

15. Compare Mr. Brown and Reverend Smith. How does the black and white thinking of Reverend Smith contribute to Umuofia's downfall? What would have prevented Umuofia's downfall?

CliffsNotes Resource Center

The learning doesn't need to stop here. CliffsNotes Resource Center shows you the best of the best—links to the best information in print and online about the author and/or related works. And don't think that this is all we've prepared for you; we've put all kinds of pertinent information at www.cliffsnotes.com. Look for all the terrific resources at your favorite bookstore or local library and on the Internet. When you're online, make your first stop www.cliffsnotes.com, where you'll find more incredibly useful information about Achebe's *Things Fall Apart*.

Books

This CliffsNotes book published by Wiley Publishing, Inc., provides a meaningful interpretation of *Things Fall Apart*. If you are looking for information about the author and/or related works, check out these other publications:

The Trouble with Nigeria, by Chinua Achebe. Portsmouth, New Hampshire: Heinemann Educational Books, Ltd., 1983. Achebe expresses his beliefs and views about the lack of leadership in Nigeria at the time of the 1983 Nigerian elections.

Chinua Achebe, by David Carroll. New York: St, Martin's Press, 1980. Carroll critiques *Things Fall Apart, No Longer at Ease, Arrow of God, A Man of the People,* short stories and poetry.

Cambridge Studies in African and Caribbean Literature, by C.L. Innes. England: Press Syndicate of the University of Cambridge, 1990. Innes compares Achebe's *Things Fall Apart* to Joyce Carey's *Mister Johnson*. Innes also writes about African and Caribbean literature as a "departure from European literary models."

Conversations with Achebe, ed, Bernth Lindfors. Jackson, Mississippi: University Press of Mississippi, 1997. Many interviews with Achebe by various authors.

Early Nigerian Literature, by Bernth Lindfors. New York: Africana Publishing Company, 1982. Early writings of authors such as Achebe (his undergraduate writings), Soyinka, Ekwensi, Tutuola, and Fafunwa.

Folklore in Nigerian Literature, by Bernth Lindfors. New York: Africana Publishing Company, 1973. A non-African reader critiques African literature.

British Policy Towards West Africa: Select Documents—1786-1874, by C.W. Newbury. Oxford, England: Clarendon Press, 1965. Original maps and copies of original documents pertaining to trade, methods of suppression, African resettlement, courts, land, finance, and customs.

Studies in Ibo Political Systems: Chieftaincy and Politics in Four Niger States, by Ikenna Nzimiro. California: University of California Press, 1972. An enlarged form of Nzimiro's doctoral thesis, which includes the ethnography and history of the Ibos, social organization, framework and functions of government, and rituals of kingship.

Chinua Achebe: A Biography, by Ezenwa Ohaeto. Bloomington, Indiana: Indiana University Press, 1997. A book about the life of Chinua Achebe.

An Introduction to the African Novel, by Eustace Palmer. New York: Africana publishing Corporation, 1972. Several African authors are discussed and critiqued. The authors include Chinua Achebe, James Ngugi, Camara Laye, Elechi Amadi, Ayi Kwei Armah, Mongo Beti, and Gabriel Okara.

Chinua Achebe, by Arthur Ravenscroft. England: Longman's, Green & Co., Ltd., 1969. Ravenscroft provides brief synopses for *Things Fall Apart, No Longer at Ease, Arrow of God,* and *A Man of the People.*

Culture and the Nigerian Novel, by Oladele Taiwo. New York: St. Martin's Press, 1976. Taiwo discusses the way African literature presents Nigerian culture and how authors link traditional beliefs and customs with modern experience.

Achebe's World: The Historical Cultural Context of the Novels, by Robert M. Wren. Washington, D.C.: Three Continents Press, Inc., 1980. Wren critiques Achebe's novels.

Internet

Check out these Web resources for more information about Chinua Achebe and *Things Fall Apart*:

The English Page, www.educeth.ch/english/readinglist/achebec/— Links to information about the author, an audio by the author, and articles about the author. This site also includes a synopsis of *Things Fall Apart* and teaching materials.

Chinua Achebe: *Things Fall Apart* Study Guide, www.wsu.edu:8000/
~brians/anglophone/achebe.html—A detailed study guide for the novel
that includes questions for each chapter. Links to information about the author
as well as other study guides are provided.

African Authors: Chinua Achebe, www.cocc.edu/cagatucci/classes/
hum211/achebe.html—An excellent site with links to information about
Achebe, Africa, African culture, African storytelling, Igbo culture and beliefs,
and *Things Fall Apart* study questions.

Chinua Achebe, www.ets.uidaho.edu/levine/achebe.html—This site
includes a biography of Achebe and a link to African studies virtual library.

Periodicals

Baker, Rob & Draper, Ellen. "If One Thing Stands, Another Will Stand Beside It."
Parabola 17 (1992): 19-28. An interview with Achebe about the storytelling
tradition in Nigeria.

Balogun, F. Odun. "Nigerian Folktales and Children's Stories By Chinua Achebe."
Journal of Black Studies 20 (1990): 426-443. Critique of Nigerian folktales and
children's stories by Achebe.

Coeyman, Marjorie. "Going Home was a Sad Awakening." *The Christian Science
Monitor* 92 (2000): 17. Achebe describes what visiting Nigeria was like after
nine years of exile.

Fleming, Bruce. "Brothers Under the Skin: Achebe on the *Heart of Darkness*." *College Literature*. 19/20 (Oct 92-Feb 93): 90-100. Fleming discusses similarities
and differences between Achebe's work and Conrad's work and how each author
defines one group through unequal references to another.

Gallagher, Susan VanZanten. "Linguistic Power: Encounter with Chinua Achebe."
The Christian Century 114 (1997): 260-261. Achebe spoke at a literary conference about *Things Fall Apart*. He wrote the book "to portray African culture
for European readers." He will not allow the book to be translated into Igbo
because Igbo is made up of many dialects.

Films and Other Recordings

A World of Ideas with Bill Moyers: Chinua Achebe. Produced and directed by Gail Pellett. Public Affairs Television, 1988, Videocassette (VHS), 28 minutes. Achebe discusses the impact of colonialism on his culture and relates that he began his own writing in reaction to certain stereotypes in Western literature.

Things Fall Apart. Recorded Books, 1997. Five unabridged cassettes, 6$\frac{1}{2}$ hours, $42.00. Read by Peter Frances James.

Send Us Your Favorite Tips

In your quest for knowledge, have you ever experienced that sublime moment when you figure out a trick that saves time or trouble? Perhaps you realized that you were taking ten steps to accomplish something that could have taken two. Or you found a little-known workaround that achieved great results. If you've discovered a useful tip that helped you understand *Things Fall Apart* more effectively and you'd like to share it, the CliffsNotes staff would love to hear from you. Go to our Web site at www.cliffsnotes.com and click the Talk to Us button. If we select your tip, we may publish it as part of CliffsNotes Daily, our exciting, free e-mail newsletter. To find out more or to subscribe to a newsletter, go to www.cliffsnotes.com on the Web.

INDEX

NOTES

NOTES

CliffsNotes

LITERATURE NOTES

CliffsNotes™
@ cliffsnotes.com

Check Out the All-New CliffsNotes Guides

TECHNOLOGY TOPICS

PERSONAL FINANCE TOPICS

CAREER TOPICS